★ ★ ★ ★ ★

'An interesting read!'

"There are a lot of interesting things in New Zealand. Like Mary Jane, I also love to travel and one of my so-called "travel-goals" is New Zealand. I often heard from my friends who have been to the country about how great it is, how fresh the air is in there and how breathtakingly beautiful the country is. In this book, Mary Jane shares her first-hand experience in New Zealand that will surely inspire readers to dream and pursue that dream to see this country. For me, this book is a sort of travel guide. You will [have] a lot of ideas as to what to do whenever [you] get the chance to visit New Zealand. I had a great time reading this book. I felt that I was already travelling there but of course, I will visit the country for real."

Joo Yoo Rin, review of initial Amazon Kindle edition, 30 March 2017

Reviews of other titles by Mary Jane Walker

'Highly Recommended'

"This person is courageous. To actually leave everything behind, pack up and go. At the same time, to be truthful, I envy her. I'm sure it took planning and skill. Most of all it took all these generous and thoughtful people to be there. At first, I thought this adventure was going to be tedious. Turns out it's different, fascinating and wonderful. This book shows all elements like where you visit, how are the people leading their lives, what is the food like, the hotels or hostels are they secure, is the staff friendly, are the people you meet honest. Overall, I enjoyed this author and am looking forward to reading her again."

Ross Knight, review of A Maverick Traveller, *initial Amazon Kindle edition, 2 February 2017*

'Awesome book and genuine writing style"

"Awesome book and genuine writing style. As a recent traveler to Cuba myself, I really appreciate how the author really embeds herself in the Cuban culture and stories that make the country so special. Great read (with great pictures). Would definitely recommend!"

Giancarlo Cozzi, review of A Maverick Cuban Way, *Amazon Kindle edition, 15 November 2017*

'Mary Jane has really outdone herself this time...”

"Wow, Mary Jane has really outdone herself this time with her best book ever. Riveting read with lots of laughs and interesting facts, you just can't put it down."

Rachel Jensen-Cable, review of A Maverick Pilgrim Way, *Amazon Kindle edition, 25 November 2017. Minor typos corrected.*

"A Maverick USA Way is a unique approach to travelling the US. Author Mary Jane Walker describes being fairly sure even before she arrived that Donald Trump would [win] and she weaves political explorations into her travels, making this much more in depth than the average travel diary... A particularly pertinent chapter covers her visit to Standing Rock... ”

Renee Jones, review of A Maverick USA Way *on Goodreads, 16 December 2017. Minor typographical corrections. All preceding reviews reproduced here were on Amazon.*

NEW ZEALAND WAY

MARY JANE WALKER

Mary Jane Walker is a writer of historically well-informed travel narratives that come with an autobiographical flavour. *A Maverick New Zealand Way* is the second book in a projected series of nine.

A light went out for Mary Jane when her mother died. She had all the possessions in the world but life was empty. So she ran away as always.

Already an experienced tramper and a budding mountaineer, Mary Jane spent time as a Department of Conservation officer, volunteering her time to build fences and set traps to protect New Zealand's rare birds on small islands, and then decided to write a book about her experiences.

So, discover the stunning scenery of New Zealand as Sir Peter Jackson did in *The Lord of the Rings* and *The Hobbit*, and many sites of Māori cultural significance as well.

In a land that spans thirteen degrees of latitude, there is a wide variety of local climates and landscapes.

Travel with Mary Jane along tracks and up mountains all over New Zealand, from Spirits Bay in the subtropical far north and the Hillary Trail on the curiously wild outskirts of Auckland, to Milford Sound and Codfish Island in the cold south; somewhere in between, explore a secret beach where penguins live among palm trees.

Mary Jane's travels around her home country reveal some truly magical locations. Not all are in the wild, because the cities of New Zealand are often picturesque and historic as well. A blend of history and trek, *A Maverick New*

Zealand Way is the perfect read to inspire you to get out and explore the land known more poetically as Aotearoa and, even, as the 'Earth's last islands.'[1]

Facebook: facebook.com/amavericktraveller
Instagram: @a_maverick_traveller
Twitter: @Mavericktravel0
Email: maryjanewalker@a-maverick.com
Linkedin: Mary Jane Walker

www.**a-maverick**.com

Other books by Mary Jane Walker

A Maverick Traveller

A Maverick Traveller is a funny, interesting adventure compilation of Mary Jane's adventures. Starting from her beginnings in travel it follows her through a life filled with exploration of cultures, mountains, histories and more. Whether it was eating dog unintentionally in Indonesia, meeting the rapper 50 Cent at a backpackers' hostel or kicking a US nuclear submarine in New Zealand, *A Maverick Traveller* is filled with the unique stories and experiences of Mary Jane Walker.

http://a-maverick.com/books/a-maverick-traveller

A Maverick Cuban Way

Trek with Mary Jane to Fidel's revolutionary hideout in the Sierra Maestra. See where the world nearly ended and the Bay of Pigs and have coffee looking at the American Guantánamo Base, all the while doing a salsa to the Buena Vista Social Club. Go to where Columbus first landed but don't expect to have wifi on your phone, only in hotspots using a card. People are proud and there's one doctor for every 150 people. Mary Jane loved it and did it.

http://a-maverick.com/books/cuban-way

A Maverick Pilgrim Way

Pilgrim trails are not just for the religious! Follow the winding ancient roads of pilgrims across the continent of Europe and the Mediterranean, and explore their hinterlands as well. Mary Jane will keep returning to complete more and more of these culturally significant routes.

http://a-maverick.com/books/pilgrim-way

A Maverick USA Way

Mary Jane took AMTRAK trains to East Glacier, West Glacier, Tetons, Estes and Yosemite national parks before the snow hit. She loved the Smithsonian museums and after seeing a live dance at the American Indian Museum, she decided to go to Standing Rock. It was a protest over land rights and drinking water, at 30 below zero! She loved Detroit which is going back to being a park, and Galveston and Birmingham, Alabama. She was there during the election and was not surprised Trump won. She was tired of being mistaken for being a homeless person because she had a backpack and left San Francisco because of it.

http://a-maverick.com/books/USA-way

A Maverick Himalayan Way   *forthcoming in 2018*

Mary Jane walked for ninety days and nights throughout the Himalayan region and Nepal, a part of the world loaded with adventures and discoveries of culture, the people, their religions and the beautiful landscapes. She visited the Hindu Kush in Pakistan and listened to the Dalai Lama in Sikkim, India. It is a journey of old and new. So, come trekking in the Himalayas with Mary Jane.

http://a-maverick.com/books/himalayan-way

A Maverick Inuit Way and the Vikings   *forthcoming in 2018*

Mary Jane's adventures in the Arctic take her dog sledding in Greenland, exploring glaciers and icebergs in Iceland, and meeting some interesting locals. She found herself stuck on a ship in the freezing Arctic Ocean amongst icebergs, and had her car windows almost blown out by gale force winds! Take a ride through the Arctic and its fascinating history.

http://a-maverick.com/books/inuit-way

A Maverick Australian Way   *forthcoming in 2018*

Mary Jane explores the diversity of Australia: sun, surf, skiing and cities! The Maverick view of Australia strongly celebrates Aboriginal culture. Mary Jane's first introduction to Australia didn't go well: she lost her job for being too friendly to an Aborigine, though that was in Queensland some time ago.

http://a-maverick.com/books/australian-way

A Maverick Middle Eastern Way   *forthcoming in 2019*

Mary Jane describes her travels in Egypt, Iran, Israel, Jordan, Palestine, the Persian Gulf, Saudi Arabia, and Turkey. Not all the Middle East is desert. Visit a land of beautiful mosques, where the culture that built the Taj Mahal originated.

http://a-maverick.com/books/mideast-way

Disclaimer

This book is a travel memoir, not an outdoors guide. Although the author and publisher have made every effort to ensure that the information in this book was correct at the time of publication, the author and publisher do not assume and hereby disclaim any liability to any party for any loss, damage, or disruption caused by errors or omissions, whether such errors or omissions result from negligence, accident, or any other cause. Some names have also been changed to disguise and protect certain individuals.

Notes on Image Sources

All maps and aerial views are credited with the original source. Abbreviations which may be used in image credits or otherwise are as follows:

DOC: New Zealand Department of Conservation

LINZ: Land Information New Zealand

NZDF: New Zealand Defence Forces

New Zealand Government material, for which Crown Copyright is otherwise reserved, is used here in accordance with published departmental Creative Commons licenses in force at the time of publication (February / March 2017).

The front cover includes an Adobe stock image by Anton Balazh, used under licence.

Contents

Spirits Bay

Rangitoto Island and Tiritiri Matangi Island

Great Barrier Island

Waipoua Forest

Coromandel and the Pinnacles

Te Aroha

The Hillary Trail

White Island

Pirongia

Taranaki, Ruapehu, Tongariro and Ngaruahoe

Waikaremoana

Abel Tasman, Cobb, Heaphy, Kahurangi and Nelson   Taranaki

St James Walkway

The Marlborough Sounds
(incl. Queen Charlotte)

Welcome Flat and Mount Cook

Kaikoura

Mount Aspiring, Gillespie,
Matukituki, Rees-Dart and Wilkin

Christchurch

Caples, Gertrude, Greenstone,
Gunn, Hollyford, Homer,
Kepler, Marian, Milford
and Routeburn

Queenstown (Latitude)

Dusky Sound

Dunedin

Hump Ridge

Codfish Island /Whenua Hou

Stewart Island / Rakiura

The Catlins

Queenstown (Longitude)

TE ARAROA

Main locations referred to in this book.

The map shown is based on NASA Earth Observatory image 2010/099.

MARY JANE WALKER

Introduction

I n the last few years, I have had some fantastic adventures. I wanted to explore, to see the world, and to write about it all.

I have now explored many parts of the world, which you can read in my other books. However, amongst all the wonders of the world, it was a story of coming home and tramping in New Zealand that I wanted to write about the most.

There are three reasons why I have written this book. The first is that I wanted to publicise the need for New Zealanders to take better care of their own backyard.

In spite of a progressive, 'clean green' image worldwide, with the national brand featuring the words '100% Pure New Zealand', the reality is that conservation in New Zealand is seriously underfunded in relation to what needs to be done to keep New Zealand pure. A country larger than Great Britain, mostly mountainous and wild and with a unique ecosystem full of introduced pests, needs serious and continuous care and attention.

The nature-conservation requirements of New Zealand are similar to the costs of upkeep of heritage in a country such as Britain or France, which every year must outlay serious money to keep the roof from leaking and replace the gilding on thousands of mansions, palaces and monuments. Conservation is to New Zealand what heritage is to many other countries.

Unfortunately, New Zealand's conservation needs create a significant strain on the national budget, given that New Zealand's population and the tax base are both roughly ten times smaller than in Britain or France. Yet by the same token a mostly wilderness-oriented form of tourism is one of New Zealand's chief export earners, in just the same way that heritage draws the tourists to Europe.

There is also a lot of 'greenwash' in New Zealand's wider environmental policies. New Zealand ratified the Paris Agreement on Climate Change in October 2016, but groundwater pollution from dairy farming, and poor urban policies, are major handicaps on this front.

If word gets out that New Zealand is less than 100% Pure in actuality, its tourism trade will suffer: as will any other New Zealand business that trades on that brand.

Another reason I wanted to write about tramping in New Zealand is because most New Zealanders do not get out to do the Great Walks. The Great Walks are New Zealand's ten premier tramping tracks. From north to south, the Great Walks are:

- Lake Waikaremoana
- Tongariro Northern Circuit
- Whanganui Journey
- Abel Tasman Coast Track
- Heaphy Track
- Paparoa Track (opening 2019)
- Routeburn Track
- Kepler Track
- Milford Track
- Rakiura Track

Department of Conservation (DOC) figures show that on some of the Great Walks, such as the Kepler Track, New Zealanders only make up a quarter of the total walkers.[2]

In addition to the Great Walks, there are many other walks and tracks, in fact far too many to mention in a single list. However, one interesting thing that DOC has done lately is to compile an additional list of New Zealand's top day-walks (as opposed to the Great Walks, which are multi-day hikes). From north to south, they are the following:

- Te Whara Track
- Cape Kidnappers Walking Track
- Tongariro Alpine Crossing
- Hooker Valley Track
- Roys Peak

These walks are described in a DOC brochure called Experience Some of our Best Day Hikes, published in October 2017. Note that the title contains the word Hikes, not Walks.

And a third reason for writing this book is that, in addition to reminding New Zealanders of what is in their own back yard and the need to look after it, I wanted to showcase New Zealand to the world.

* * *

For a long time, I used to take my holidays overseas, and ignore what was in my own backyard in New Zealand. Many New Zealanders get into this habit, which is pretty ironic when you consider how many tourists come halfway around the world to visit New Zealand. The grass is always greener, I suppose.

What spurred me to get back into the Kiwi outdoors was the beginnings of a mid-life crisis, I suppose you would call it, which needed to be overcome with some exercise therapy. In 2010 my mother died of Alzheimer's Disease. A light went out for me in Auckland then; and it was during this time that Graham Ure, my life coach, told me that he knew a lot of women my age who were taking antidepressants.

At that moment, I realised that life is too short to be sitting around wondering what to do next or what man you're going to meet. I thought that if you live your life assuming you're going to meet someone, or that something is going to change, nothing will change. Unless you can find something strong within yourself, there won't be any change.

I was in my early forties with everything I wanted — my own business, three cars, five TV sets — but I thought, well, why? Why have so many things when really, I wasn't particularly happy? If I didn't change my life, I was going to end up like a lot of other people: strung out on antidepressants.

I decided that I wasn't going to have a mid-life crisis. And so, I rediscovered the pastime of tramping in New Zealand, after planting seventy native trees in my suburban Auckland home. All this gardening made me realise that I wasn't cut out for city life and that my childhood had instilled a passion for the wilder parts of New Zealand in me. The trouble with Auckland is that an attractive, indeed fabulous, natural setting of the kind that is typical of New Zealand has been trashed by traffic, ugly buildings, and a general air of impatience (mostly due to the traffic).

I will in fact be devoting the longest chapter of this book, plus a couple of others, to some of the 'green' areas indicated in the NASA satellite photograph above: to Rangitoto Island; to a popular tramping route rugged

Auckland in its Fabulous Natural Setting (North to Left).

Source: Detail from Nasa Earth Observatory jpeg image
Auckland_17_2002239, taken 27 August 2002

The 'Queen City', or, Auckland As It Used To Be: Grafton Gully, 29 January 1949. The urban wilderness trail shown here, at a location near the inner-city waterfront and leading down to it, was taken for a motorway in the 1960s.

Source: Detail from 'Grafton Road, Auckland', Whites Aviation Ltd: Photographs. Ref: WA-19229-F. Alexander Turnbull Library, Wellington, New Zealand. http://natlib.govt. nz/recors/22512926

Auckland Now: 'Spaghetti Junction' from Hopetoun Street. It's usually more congested than this, by the way. Photo: Chris Harris

Coromandel area of which a part appears on the extreme east end of the photo (the top); and, at greatest length, to Auckland's own wild west coast at the bottom.

But the city itself now leaves something to be desired in comparison to the days when it was known as the 'Queen City' of the South Pacific, when areas such as Grafton Gully had not yet been paved over for the motorway.

On the other hand, in provincial areas of New Zealand like Hastings where I grew up, life is still the way it was in the 1950s in a lot of ways. While that implies a certain measure of backwardness it also means less traffic and worry. And that is really the medium I seek.

So, I decided to get on with my life, using travel and trekking outside of Auckland as my stimulation. Although he was a great supporter of mine, I don't think even Graham could quite believe it when I started tramping and then suddenly just moved away from Auckland. I tried living in several places before settling in Queenstown, where I now live for a part of the year – the world is my home the rest of the year. Even though I'd been all over the world, I thought that New Zealand was the most beautiful country on

Earth – I still do – and decided I had a lot to do here in my home country before I went overseas again.

And so, I was impelled to wander once more, but in New Zealand this time.

* * *

While most of the chapters of this book describe tramps and rambles in New Zealand's great outdoors, it is worth noting that New Zealand has many fine urban areas that are worth exploring too. Moreover, New Zealand is an urban nation in the habits and occupations of its people. According to the latest, 2013, census, 87 per cent of New Zealanders are urbanites, a percentage that is actually higher than in many Northern Hemisphere countries. Most New Zealanders live in cities; and most of those cities are on the coast.

For many New Zealanders, their everyday experience of life is of a sort of Riviera, of a kind that can be seen in many cities and coastal towns. Examples of such cities and towns include Wellington; Napier and the neighbouring, somewhat more inland city Hastings where I grew up, both rebuilt in a 1930s 'Art Deco' style following a 1931 earthquake; New Plymouth; Timaru, Oamaru and Dunedin. Auckland itself was known as the 'Queen City', the Queen of the South Pacific, for the same reason.

The experience of living in a coastal Riviera was even more common in the mid-twentieth century, when the photographs immediately below were taken. Unfortunately, New Zealand's port cities have since sprawled inland in the form of soul-less and ticky-tacky suburbs, on the American model.

As the earlier photograph captioned 'The Queen City' suggests, the most obvious problem in Auckland is the sacrifice of such a Riviera-like downtown

Wellington: Oriental Bay, 22 December 1959.

Source: Oriental Bay, Wellington City. Negatives of the Evening Post newspaper. Ref: EP/1959/4347-F. Alexander Turnbull Library, Wellington, New Zealand. http://natlib.govt.nz/records/30649458. Cropped to remove extraneous sky from original square-format image.

to the sinuous coils of the so-called Spaghetti Junction, a motorway junction which is not only unsightly but also a magnet for suburban traffic of the kind that would otherwise have gone around the central city, and for inner-area car-commuters whose needs would better have been served by railways, ferries, trams and buses.

From a clogged and despoiled centre, congestion then radiates outward along Auckland's motorways all the way to quite distant suburbs.

Paradoxically, a tendency to worship the great outdoors has led New Zealanders to neglect the cities in which they live and their own civic

Anti-littering campaign billboard on Karangahape Road, central Auckland, 2011. Photography by Patrick Reynolds.

backyard. The latter includes natural areas close to, and even within, the city itself: from Auckland's wild west coast to the now-destroyed Grafton Gully.

For me, this issue is summed up in a nutshell by an urban anti-littering billboard that appeared on Auckland's Karangahape Road a few years ago, showing a venturesome mountain biker above Queenstown, where I now live, in the southern lakes region of the South Island, with the legend, 'Why we love NZ' (New Zealand). We love NZ, so don't drop litter.

Somehow the dismal inner city carpark underneath, though closer to Auckland's urban reality, wasn't seen to be the 'real' New Zealand and an image of a much more remote area was used instead. It was as if an anti-littering campaign in London used an image of the Scottish Highlands!

While *A Maverick New Zealand Way* is mostly about the more remote parts of New Zealand's outdoors and the many great opportunities that exist in this country to escape from the city into the wilderness, I have deliberately tried to balance the book not only with chapters on Auckland's backyard but also with a chapter called 'Towns, Traditions and Gardens' which is even more focused on urban areas as such. That chapter appears in the South Island section of the book since it is mostly about the cities of the South Island and their unusually fine Victorian heritage, though it touches on Auckland as well. I also have chapters that discuss the Christchurch earthquakes, the city of Dunedin, and Queenstown.

It would be a good thing if we could be as passionate about our cities and our civic backyard as we are about the more remote parts of the New Zealand outdoors. Then New Zealand really could claim to be the best place in the world to live, work, play and visit.

11

MY TRAMPING GEAR LIST (TWO PAGES)

Gear	*Food Suggestions
• Backpack (about 70L)	• Scroggin (mixed nuts& dried fruit)
• Plastic liner (essential)	
• Travel towel (small)	• Dried meals (I like Kathmandu, a New Zealand brand)
• Raincoat	
• Over-pants (preferably waterproof)	
• Warm hat	• Couscous
• Gloves	• Camembert & Cheddar cheese
• Sun hat	
• Shorts	• Marmite/jam/chutney in film containers
• Hand gel	
• Lip balm	• Hot chocolate/cappuccino sachets
• Survival bag	
• Sunblock	• Tea bags
• Insect repellent	• Muesli/porridge
• Crocs or light hut shoes	• Instant custard mix
• Torch (preferably a head torch)	• Mashed potato (dried)
• Long johns, x2	• Soup mix
• Woollen socks (one pair per day)	• Dried vegetables
• Boots	• Cuisine rice
• Sleeping bag	• Crackers/pita breads
• Wool singlet, x2	• Dates and dried apple, mango& apricots
• Wool t-shirt, x2	
• Long sleeve wool top, x1 or 2	• Milk powder
• Fleece top, x2	• Gluten-free falafel mix (with rice and Thai chilli sauce!)
• Underwear	
• Sunglasses	

- Camera
- Stove
- Cooking gas
- 1.25L water
- First-aid kit including blister Band-Aids
- Lighter & waterproof matches
- Food*
- Billy, mug, bowl, spoon and sharp knife
- Snap-lock bags for food
- Plastic bags to divide clothes etc.
- Toilet paper
- Toiletries, small and light
- Dishwashing liquid & a small pot scrubber
- Pack cover (useful if it rains)
- Compass, survival kit& whistle
- Map
- Puttees or gaiters (optional)
- Strips of rubber
- Rope
- Pocket knife
- Orthotics/soles/Vaseline/wool to wrap around toes
- Thin cloths cut in two, for washing self and dishes
- Waistband with pockets
- Cheap reading glasses
- Candle

- Packet of sweet-and-sour sauce mix and pine nuts
- Eggs
- Miso soups and instant packet soups
- Hard boiled eggs
- Energy drinks, eg. Hairy Lemon sachets
- Packet biscuits – don't bother about pudding
- Marshmallows

Some food can be shared amongst the group as well!

NATIONAL PARKS IN NEW ZEALAND

1. Tongariro
2. Egmont
3. Whanganui
4. Kahurangi
5. Abel Tasman
6. Nelson Lakes
7. Paparoa
8. Arthur's Pass
9. Westland / Tai Poutini
10. Aoraki / Mt Cook
11. Mt Aspiring
12. Fiordland
13. Rakiura

Note:

Until recently there was a fourteenth national park, Te Urewera National Park, but it was disestablished as a national park in 2014 and renamed simply Te Urewera – a statutory entity – after being returned to indigenous stewardship under the Tūhoe Māori iwi, or tribe.

(The map graphic above was sources from the DOC website on 12 December 2016)

14

THE TOTAL CONSERVATION ESTATE

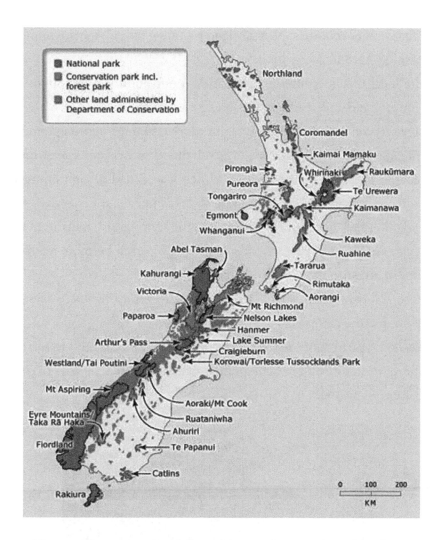

This graphic was sourced from *Te Ara, the Encyclopaedia of New Zealand*, on 12 December 2016, where it appears under the title 'Land Administered by the Department of Conservation, 2007'. Note that Te Urewera is still included as a National Park, a status that is now out of date for reasons explained on the preceding page.

MANAGING MASS TOURISM (WHY IT PAYS TO BOOK!)

Like many other countries, New Zealand is finding today's tourism numbers increasingly hard to accommodate.

The local media regularly run stories about pollution in supposedly pristine area and a general need to manage access better.

One very topical issue these days is 'freedom camping', meaning camping outside approved campgrounds. In 2011 the New Zealand Government passed the Freedom Camping Act, which was aimed at tightening up controls on the roughly 150,000 campers who camped in this way each year.

Old, informal, arrangements that suited the less intensive tourism of fifty years ago are falling by the wayside and being replaced by more regulated systems of access to the New Zealand experience.

As such it pays to check and book as far ahead as possible these days, lest you find that the best places are taken.

Just as in other countries, local attractions may also be subject to seasonal closure, or to closure by a natural disaster such as a landslide. It pays to check for these reasons, too.

Cruise liner in Doubtful Sound (Fiordland National Park), January 2018. Photo by Chris Harris.

A NOTE ON MAPS AND IMAGES

Note: If you have a copy of this book in which the images are printed in black and white, or if you have a Kindle with a black-and-white screen, you can see all of the images in this book that were originally in colour, in full colour, on the author's website http://a-maverick.com, behind a button that looks like this: 🖼 Preview with Colour Images

The maps that appear in this book have been drawn from a variety of sources, including two key government sources, the New Zealand Department of Conservation (DOC) and Land Information New Zealand (LINZ). Bar one exception, all maps, aerial photos and satellite images are shown with north at the top. The exception is the satellite image of Auckland that appears on page 5. All image captions are rasterised, which means that they stay with the image in Kindle and similar programs, but that web addresses contained in the captions are not clickable.

Readers are in every case urged to make use of original maps (often zoomable if online) and guides when in the outdoors; the maps and aerial/satellite images shown in this book are purely for illustration. For a literally more all-round perspective, you might also wish to look at some of localities I describe – like this one – in the 3D view on Google Earth.

Intersection of the Wilkin river and Siberia Stream, South Island, looking northward. Google Earth Screenshot in 3D view. Imagery ©2017 DigitalGlobe, Map data ©2017 Google.

PART I
THE NORTH ISLAND

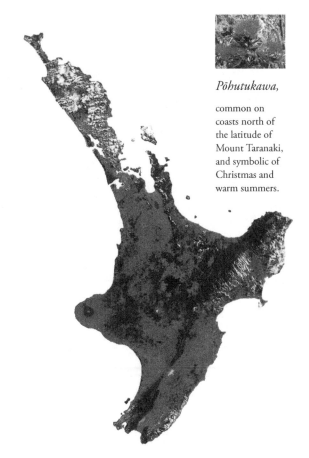

Pōhutukawa,

common on
coasts north of
the latitude of
Mount Taranaki,
and symbolic of
Christmas and
warm summers.

The North Island of New Zealand

Source: detail from the NASA Earth Observatory image 2010/099

CHAPTER ONE
Spirits Bay and Sand Duning

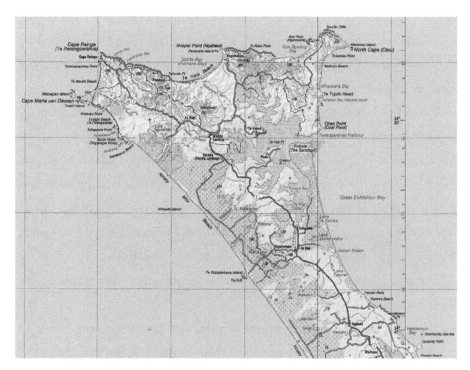

The very northernmost tip of the North Island of New Zealand
(LINZ via NZTopomaps.com)

S PIRITS Bay is in the far north of New Zealand, with subtropical white sandy beaches and fabulous sunrises and sunsets. While well worth exploring on its own merits, this beautiful area also serves as the starting point for the Te Paki Coastal Track. This is a 48 km walk of three to four days, which also takes in Cape Reinga, also known as Te Rerenga Wairua, where the Pacific Ocean and Tasman Sea meet.

Cape Reinga/Te Rerenga Wairua, which is about halfway along the track, is a sacred place and in Māori mythology is considered to be the place where the spirits of the dead go to be cleansed and then leap off and enter the underworld to return to their home of Hawaiki-a-Nui.[3] Te Rerenga Wairua means 'the place where the spirits fly' and Reinga means 'underworld'.[4]

A little more than 220 km north of Kaitaia, Spirits Bay is reached by turning off State Highway 1 at Waitiki Landing onto Te Hapua Road, and then turning left onto Spirits Bay Road.[5]

When I did the tramp in April, the availability of water was of concern. As DOC notes, the streams on the trail can dry out over summer,[6] so we had to have the capacity to carry 4 litres of water each to make sure we had enough to last the tramp. We were camping as we went and stayed first at Spirits Bay (Kapowairua) Campsite and from there walked 18 km to Tapotupotu Bay, north of Spirits Bay. The next place we stayed at was Te Werahi Beach, about 7 km on, and then walked on another 10 km to Te Paki Stream where we came out onto the immense sand dunes which people often boogie board on.

The track was varied in its vegetation and density, but mostly it was an easy walk. However, I found out how easily even an experienced camper could set a forest on fire – which has happened before – as I almost set the tent alight when we pitched it in the kikuyu grass (which, by the way, makes an amazing mattress – you don't even really need to bring one) on the first few nights and I was cooking dinner.

I don't always like going around the coast without bush for cover, but you can't always have bush as a lot of New Zealand has been cleared historically. I found the grassy sections quite difficult, but the coastal walk was still well worth it.

Above: Tatopotu Campground and whale skeleton

An easy tramp!

Spirits Bay beaches

23

Some more scenes, including the Cape Reinga Lighthouse

Sand Boarding at Te Paki Stream, and two views of Cape Maria van Diemen with the twin humps of Motupao Island beyond

The lonely sea and sky

Road flooding

Beach campfire

*Crossing
a stream*

CHAPTER TWO

The 'Winterless North'

WAIPOUA FOREST, THE BAY OF ISLANDS AND CAPE BRETT

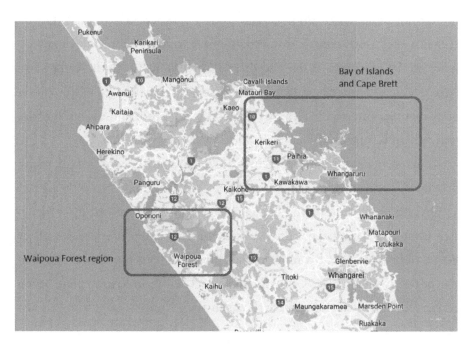

Waipoua Forest, the Bay of Islands and Cape Brett

Red boxes and names of Bay of Islands and Cape Brett added for this book. Map data ©2018 Google.

S OUTH of the long, thin peninsula that leads to Cape Reinga and Spirits Bay is the main bulk of the part of New Zealand known as Northland, a region long dubbed the 'winterless north' by local tourism operators. This is almost true, even if it isn't literally true.

For Northland is sub-tropical and supports the growing of fruit that won't grow anywhere else in New Zealand such as cherimoya, or 'custard apples'. It is a stronghold of Māori culture and has many beautiful, typically Polynesian beaches with jagged islands offshore for a backdrop. It was also the first place to be settled by Europeans in New Zealand.

British settlers sought to log the region's extensive rainforests, within which the most prized species was the kauri (*Agathis australis*), a survivor of a group of ancient, dinosaur-age conifers; a member of a family that contains the South American monkey-puzzle tree, the Norfolk Pine, and other species of kauri that live elsewhere in the Pacific. Of all these, the kauri were esteemed as particularly valuable to loggers, partly because the oldest ones are huge and partly because the wood is rot-proof and easy to work as well, with a beautiful, honey-like appearance.

Kauri also produce hard resin called kauri gum, which had many decorative and industrial uses at one time.

On the other side of the ledger, kauri also have enormous spiritual significance to Māori. That did not prevent their plunder; though as they began to become scarce a more conservation-minded mood took hold in the population at large. Unfortunately, as I will go on to explain, even conserved kauri now face a new threat in the form of a condition known as kauri dieback disease.

After the logging of the kauri, Northland struggled to find new industries In fact, lack of opportunity means that Northland is also the capital of a booming marijuana-cultivation industry: another exotic crop to add to the list. (This may all soon become legal in New Zealand, though less of a money-spinner.)

One thing I noticed was how much effort was being put into kiwi sanctuaries in the area. According to the website 'Kiwis for Kiwi', "Northland is one of the hotspots for community-led kiwi groups."[7] The site lists eight community-led kiwi conservation efforts north of Auckland, and there are public sanctuaries at Russell and Whangarei; perhaps there will be more by the time you read this.

Northland is steeped in Māori history and there are many old urupā, or graveyards, disgorging skeletal remains (kōiwi tangata) as a consequence of the erosion of sandy soil. The New Zealand Historic Places trust has a leaflet on what to do with them if encountered (which is, basically, to not interfere and to call the police just in case).

In the current chapter I take a look at the remaining kauri stronghold of the Waipoua Forest on the west coast, and at the marine playground of the Bay of Islands and its protective southern breakwater, the Cape Brett peninsula, on the east coast.

The Cape Brett peninsula is also of great significance to Māori, as the supposed branching-off place of the seven ancestral ocean-going canoes (double-hulled and more like catamaran yachts) on which the ancestors of the Māori were said to have arrived from Hawaiki, that is to say, Eastern Polynesia, roughly one thousand years ago. In the traditional story, the vessels arrived at the peninsula and then split up to settle different parts of New Zealand.

The Waipoua Forest, and the Bay of Islands and nearby Cape Brett, are just two places worth visiting in Northland. There's plenty more to this slow-paced region, which, in spite of its natural beauty and proximity to Auckland, still provides a range of fairly uncrowded and uncommercial experiences. Some other parts of New Zealand, such as Queenstown, are starting to become quite busy with international tourists. That isn't true of Northland – yet.

THE TALLEST GIANT: TĀNE MAHUTA AND THE WAIPOUA FOREST

Waipoua Forest is home to Tāne Mahuta, the tallest kauri tree in the world. Named after the god of the forest, Tāne Mahuta is over fifty metres tall and just under four and a half metres in diameter. Thought to be about two thousand years old, this immense tree is one of several impressive sights in the forest. These also include the second tallest kauri, Te Matua Ngahere which means The Father of the Forest.[8]

Located in Northland, Waipoua Forest makes up the largest remaining tract of native bush in the area together with the adjoining forests of Mataraua and Waima. At only 65 km from Dargaville, it can be easily reached by car via State Highway 12, which runs through the forest.[9] I took Niels, a French friend of mine, there to see the majestic kauri, which are absolute giants. Looking up at the huge tree, you can see how Tāne Mahuta got its name. The god Tāne Mahuta is also considered in Māori mythology to be the child who broke the embrace of the sky father, Ranginui and earth mother, Papatuanuku, thus allowing light into the world.[10]

We may not have the Eiffel Tower in New Zealand, but we do have some of the oldest and tallest trees in the world. We need to protect these, as well as the kiwi, which are steadily dying out on the mainland due to predation. For this reason, we need the Hauraki Gulf islands such as Tiritiri Matangi, just out of Auckland, to serve as reserves dedicated to rebuilding the endangered species of birds and certain trees. On islands such as Tiritiri Matangi, about which I will have more to say below, volunteers trap predators and species are monitored. Who knows, perhaps one day the tallest kauri might come from there? But until then, it can be found right here on the mainland in Waipoua Forest.

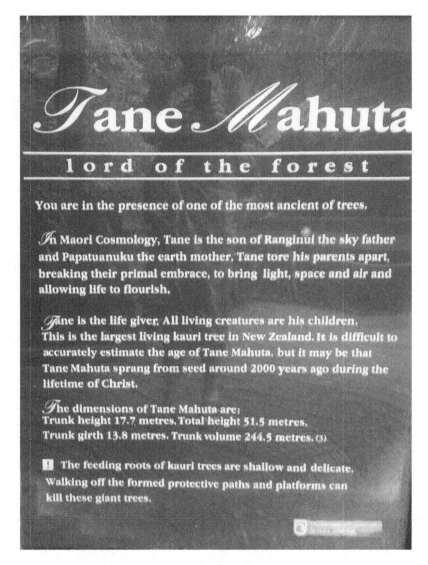

Tāne Mahuta sign

One thing I noticed at Waipoua was the growing prevalence of dead and dying kauri, the consequence of kauri dieback disease. And, alongside, growing evidence of official attempts to deal with the problem.

Waipoua Signs

Kauri Dieback

Kauri dieback disease is caused by a fungus-like organism which lives in water and soil and is called phytophthora, meaning 'destroyer of plants'.

The problem has been known since 1974. However, past outbreaks of kauri dieback (a word which means loss of upper foliage) were minor.

The latest outbreak, gathering pace since 2006, is more virulent. The kauri don't just die back now, but die completely. The variety that is attacking the kauri right now was probably introduced from a foreign country, meaning that the kauri have little immunity.

Treatment can save juvenile kauri from the new dieback. But it is less practical for the giants of the forest.

For a while, the strategy for coping with the new outbreak consisted of boot-washing stations at the entrances and exits of tracks in affected areas. It was hoped that all visitors would voluntarily disinfect their footwear, and thereby stop the plague from spreading further.

Both beliefs now seem touchingly optimistic, and steadily more extreme controls on access and movement are being introduced.

Kauri dieback is not the only plague to hit New Zealand's native vegetation, which was isolated from the outside world for millions of years and consequently lacks immunity. For instance, a South American fungus known in English as myrtle rust has spread around the Pacific to Australia, where it was found in 2010, and has now crossed the Tasman to New Zealand.

The most visible potential victims of myrtle rust in New Zealand, almost on a par with the kauri in terms of their cultural and sentimental significance, are New Zealand's several species of rātā and their northern coastal cousin, the pōhutukawa.

Wild pōhutukawa and rātā flower with red blossoms at Christmas and add to the sense of festivity. In fact, the pōhutukawa-in-bloom is the number-one symbol of a New Zealand Christmas.

And so, the second decade of the 21st century has revealed what may be a series of potential extinction events for iconic New Zealand tree species.

In the earliest days of the Māori settlement of New Zealand, the giant flightless birds called moa were wiped out by over-hunting. Ka ngaro i te ngaro a te moa, 'lost as the moa is lost', became a Māori expression of regret.

May we yet see the kauri and the pōhutukawa join the moa, I wonder?

Ka ngaro? Pōhutukawa in bloom at Cornwallis Beach, Auckland
Public domain image by Ed323, Wikimedia Commons (9 January 2008)

Tāne Mahuta

Tāne Mahuta

Some smaller neighbouring kauri, in the light

Te Matua Ngahere, 'the father of the forest'

THE BAY OF ISLANDS AND CAPE BRETT

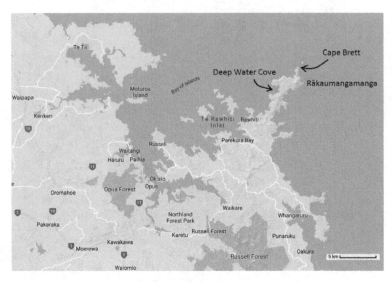

Bay of Islands, Cape Brett peninsula, and environs. Names of Cape Brett,
Deep Water Cove and Rākaumangamanga added for this book.

Map data ©2018 Google.

Sign showing the Cape Brett Track. Rākaumangamanga refers to
a seven-peak mountain or hill at the end of the peninsula.

One of the most famous places in New Zealand is the Bay of Islands. As its name suggests, this gorgeous bay on the east coast of Northland, due north-east of Waipoua Forest, is full of islands. It is shielded from cold southern winds, any that make it this far north, by Cape Brett.

The Bay of Islands is fairly touristy these days, though not as touristy as some other places in New Zealand. For a long time, the Bay of Islands attracted domestic holidaymakers, as well as wealthy visitors intent on catching big fighting fish such as Marlin. The American author Zane Grey wrote about the place in the 1920s, popularising it in a book called *Tales of the Angler's El Dorado*.

Before that, the Bay of Islands was the seat of New Zealand's very first capital at Russell; and is the site of the Treaty House, where the founding Treaty of Waitangi was signed on the 6th of February, 1840, between Queen Victoria's representatives and a number of Māori rangatira, or chieftains.

With global warming, the area north of Auckland is slated to become more tropical. It is lashed from time to time by cyclones, and this is likely

This is not where I stayed (but pretty close nearby)

41

to get worse. However, between storms, it's a lovely part of Polynesia. That's particularly true of sheltered east coast areas like the Bay of Islands.

I stopped in first of all at the Bland Bay Motor Camp near Whangaruru, which is toward the bottom right of the map just above. This area, south of the Cape Brett peninsula, is a refuge from the busier and more commercialised Bay of Islands proper.

The Bland Bay Motor Camp is run by the Ngāti Wai iwi, or tribal group.[11] I went for beautiful walks around Bland Bay and nearby Puriri Bay. I stayed there for three days just relaxing, but then I thought that I had to take up the challenge of hiking the length of the Cape Brett peninsula toward its jagged, seven-peaked tip known as Rākaumangamanga.

The Māori word rākau means tree or stick, while manga means branch. Doubling up the word manga adds emphasis. The significance of Rākaumangamanga is that it is by Māori tradition, as rendered into English, 'the branching-off place of the canoes'.

Rākaumangamanga

The canoes are the ones by which the Polynesian ancestors of the Māori arrived. Although later canoes of the New Zealand Māori were single-hulled and propelled by paddles, the vessels on which their ancestors arrived in New Zealand would have been sailing catamarans: a common type in island Polynesia.

As the story has it, New Zealand was colonised by seven canoes. The seven canoes, or catamarans, are supposed to have arrived jointly at Cape Brett in a fleet and then gone on separate ways around New Zealand, dropping off colonists at suitable locations. The seven peaks of Rākaumangamanga thus represent the original colonising fleet.

However many vessels there were in actuality, and whether they all came at once or not, the legend's theme of a deliberate and organised process of colonisation is backed up by modern research.

The ancestors of the Polynesians lived on islands off the Asian coast, where they were related to other island peoples such as the majority of the inhabitants of Java, and the indigenous people of Taiwan.

The Polynesians gradually spread eastward into the Pacific Ocean and became very accomplished and deliberate ocean navigators and colonists. The islands of New Zealand were merely the last and largest islands to be colonised by Polynesian people; who also frequently called themselves Māori, or a similar word. This meant ordinary or common, as opposed to other peoples that the Polynesians sometimes met such as the Europeans who began arriving, in earnest, in the eighteenth century.

The islands of New Zealand would have been the most challenging to colonise, since they were well south of the main latitudes of Polynesia, with different wind patterns and colder seas. So, the Māori colonisation of New Zealand could have required a particularly organised expedition, or series of expeditions.

With regard to hiking the Cape Brett peninsula – where the whole human history of New Zealand is thus said to have begun – the first thing to mention is that the track takes about eight hours from start to finish.

In several places it gets gnarly and exposed, with big drop-offs to either side, though the views are terrific.

The track is graded as 'advanced' in Department of Conservation literature, which falls short of mountaineering but does mean that it is a good idea to be kitted out with boots and hiking poles and proper tramping gear all round, along with having a reasonable level of fitness and a head for heights.[12] The track is not open to mountain bikers, because it is actually too steep and (potentially) dangerous for that.

There are several carparks at the beginning. A lot of cars get robbed, though you can pay $8, currently, for more secure parking. The first section runs along Māori communal land, and then you get into conservation areas. There is a stream and a water tank half along the track, but carrying water is recommended. I would recommend carrying water purification pills as well.

The remarkable Whangamumu Bay, guarded between two natural breakwaters

You can make side-trips from the main track to the old Whangamumu Bay whaling station and other areas of interest. Whangamumu Bay is well worth it, a white sand beach sheltered by two peninsulas that act as natural breakwaters.

Nīkau Palms and toilet with a view, overlooking Deep Water Cove

A less obstructed view of the islands of the Bay of Islands,
as seen from Deep Water Cove

Further along, you get to Deep Water Cove on the western side, which has terrific views of the Bay of Islands. This also be enjoyed from a strategically-located toilet, though only with the door open of course.

For those who don't want parking hassles or too long a walk, it's possible to take a water taxi from various Bay of Islands localities such as Russell, Paihia and Oke Bay to Deep Water Cove or Cape Brett. One advantage of taking the water taxi all the way to or from Cape Brett is that if sea conditions allow, the taxi may go through the famous 'Hole in the Rock' at Motukōkako (Piercy Island) just off Cape Brett.

The water taxi costs $50 per person to or from Cape Brett at the time of publication, or $40 to or from Deep Water Cove, but minimum per-boat

The 'hole in the rock' through Motukōkako (Piercy Island), with Oruwhanga Island and Cape Brett behind.

By Matt Lemmon on Wikimedia Commons, CC-BY-SA 2.0, 12 January 2008.

Cape Brett Lighthouse with Otuwhanga Island to the left and Motukōkako (Piercy Island) and Tiheru Island behind

The smaller Tiheru Island is in front of Motukōkako. Motu means island in Māori, so to say Motukōkako Island would be a double-up.

Myself by the Cape Brett Lighthouse and islands

47

Cape Brett Hut with Otuwhanga Island in the background

A striking sunset, with shadows of low clouds on the clouds above, from a hill beside the Cape Brett Hut

charges apply, i.e. it must have a quorum of passengers (about five), or else the rate per person goes up.[13]

Near the Cape Brett Lighthouse is the so-called Cape Brett Hut, overlooked by the massive looming presence of Otuwhanga Island. Rather flash as huts go, it used to be the lighthouse keeper's house, of course.

It's necessary to book the hut in advance if you want to stay there. It has a combination lock, and you get the combination on booking. Currently, the fee is $15 a night for an adult (18+), half-price for those 11-17. Younger children are free.

I saw a stoat running along the track. Fingers of land like the Cape Brett peninsula are obvious candidates for being fenced off and made predator-free. It's a sign of DOC funding stress that they aren't.

There is also a fee for walking across the Māori land, which goes toward he maintenance of the track on that section. The fee is currently $40 per adult or $20 per child. The fee is paid on the Department of Conservation website. The website capebrett.co.nz notes that the arrangements for paying the fee on the DOC website are rather confusing and provides helpful tips on how to get it right.[14]

The fee can also be avoided by taking the water taxi both ways, though this means missing out on a portion of the track. In an ideal world the private owners would be fully compensated by DOC, but I suspect that neither the department's budget nor, perhaps, its present organisational capabilities run to that.

Postscript: There is an excellent Youtube video called 'Cape Brett Track – Living a Kiwi Life – Ep. 45' which has been recommended by New Zealand's Department of Conservation, and which gives a very good idea of what the track is like, including the exposed bits which may not be for everyone.[15]

CHAPTER THREE
Great Barrier Island

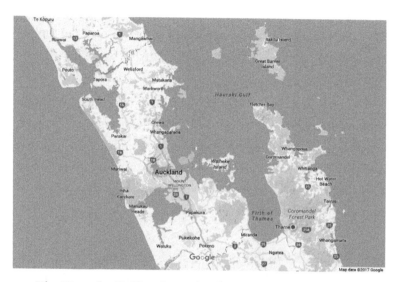

The Hauraki Gulf and its Islands. Map Data ©2017 Google.

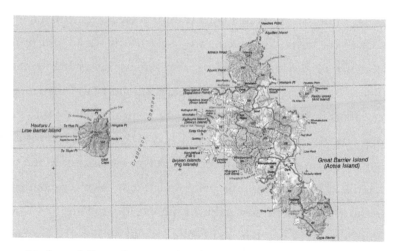

Little and Great Barrier Islands. LINZ via NZTopomaps (2017).

L ARGEST of Auckland's Hauraki Gulf Islands is Great Barrier Island, also known as Aotea, the island of the white cloud or the shining sky. When I get tele-marketing calls selling holidays on Australia's Great Barrier Reef, I tell them, 'We have our own Great Barrier Island.' I don't tell them it's not so big!

Nor is it as polluted. Great Barrier Island comes in near the top of coastal destinations rated by *National Geographic* in 2010:

Only 55 miles of ocean separate Great Barrier Island from cosmopolitan Auckland, but given how little the two places have in common, the distance seems much greater. With less than 1,000 permanent residents, more than half of its land area administered by New Zealand's Department of Conservation, and fewer introduced species than elsewhere in the country, the island is in good shape ecologically and will likely remain so for a while.[16]

Located 90 km (55 miles) north-east of Auckland on the edge of the Hauraki Gulf Marine Park, New Zealand's 'National Park of the Sea', the island can be reached by a 4-hour ferry ride, or a scenic half-hour flight.

In 1993, I bought shares in a bach (cabin) there along with a few other people. Over the years, I've loved going over to the island and tramping the 621-metre high Mount Hobson, also known by its Māori name of Hirakimata, as well as visiting other parts of the island. There are no possums, stoats or ferrets on the island, which means that despite the few remaining rats the forest is largely untouched. The island is beautiful, with jagged green mountains like those seen on Polynesian islands in the tropics and huge nīkau palms – the only palm endemic to New Zealand (in two species) and the southernmost palm in the world, growing to 44 degrees south. Furthermore, Great Barrier or Aotea Island is so off the beaten track that it doesn't really get a lot of city slickers and is the perfect place to get away for a break.

New Zealand conservation revolves to a large extent around the control of introduced pests. For instance, an estimated 70 million individuals of the introduced Australian brushtail possum species, *Trichosurus vulpecula* – 'the little foxy one with the brush-tail', which makes it sound extra cute – are thought to consume 21 thousand tonnes of New Zealand bush a night (brushtail possums are nocturnal).[17] They also eat baby or juvenile birds, as do other introduced mammalian pests such as rats, ferrets and stoats. On top of that brushtail possums also spread diseases such as bovine tuberculosis, putting the farmer at risk. Thus, possums have few friends in New Zealand. Fortunately, "Great Barrier Island is free of possums, stoats, ferrets, weasels, Norway rats, hedgehogs, deer and feral goats."[18]

This is mainly a consequence of its isolation; it is an offence nowadays to transport such creatures around the Hauraki Gulf lest they make landfall on Great Barrier, or on even more highly protected islands such as Little Barrier Island.[19]

Whale Sighting off Great Barrier Island

*Blind Bay, in
front of Okupu*

Windy Canyon

The bay at Okiwi

*The author at the Kaitoke
Hot Pools*

*The Kaitoke
Hot Pools*

On the beach at Awana

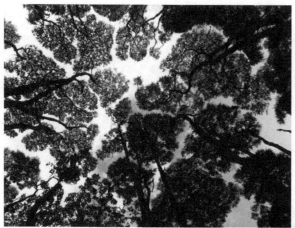

Some of the patterns of nature on Great Barrier Island

At Mount Heale Hut (of which more below), I came across a December 2014 *New Yorker* article ('The big kill: New Zealand's crusade to rid itself of mammals'), which claimed that New Zealand conservation was mostly a matter of calling in the exterminators. The *New Yorker* article gives a rather negative impression of the humanity of this approach. However, a more recent article in the *New Zealand Listener* by Rebecca Macfie, 'Natural born killers', 26 November 2016, makes clear that many of the introduced predators in New Zealand experience boom and bust cycles; if they are not poisoned, they will starve, after first eating as much of the native bush and wildlife as possible.

Certainly, our methods are working to the extent that the funding and resources (often volunteer resources) are available. Great Barrier Island had been partly cleared of its trees by pests such as possums, and is only now regenerating after all the work the volunteers have done in wiping out the pests. In the long run the scientists would prefer a species-specific contraceptive, but so far that has not yet been developed. Another article by Rebecca Macfie in the 3 December 2016 issue of the *New Zealand Listener* follows up on such long-term solutions.

Although Great Barrier Island and other Hauraki Gulf islands missed out on getting the worst mammalian pests, they are often still home to smaller species of rats and mice. At the moment, there are plans to exterminate all the remaining rodent pests on nearby Rakitu or Arid Island using brodifacoum, so that the island can be re-populated by native species, which of course evolved in the complete absence of mammals other than two species of bat.[20]

Alongside government conservation efforts, at Port Fitzroy, on the western shore of the island, there is also a private conservation sanctuary called Glenfern, founded by the late Auckland yachtsman Tony Bouzaid.

Glenfern Sanctuary Signs

Port Fitzroy

Tony Bouzaid
Monument
above Port
Fitzroy

VIEWS AND POOLS

Several of the most popular destinations on the island are on a scenic trail known as the Aotea Track. These include the peak of Hirakimata, and Windy Canyon, a *Lord of the Rings* filming site, I walked a part of the Aotea Track in January 2015 with my friend Rose and her partner, Daniel. We hiked along it to the top of Hirakimata, where there are amazing 360-degree views of the island. There are also free hot pools located on a section of the track that leads from the Whangaparapara Road to Hirakimata: the Kaitoke hot pools.

At that time, I wasn't able to hike all of the Aotea Track because of damage from a June 2014 storm, which tragically struck just as the track had been upgraded. However, the Aotea Track was fully re-opened in 2016, so everything is back to normal.

In 2015, meanwhile, the New Zealand Government also created the Aotea Conservation Park to oversee the Aotea Track and other Great Barrier Island conservation resources. The Park's advisory body, the Aotea Conservation Park Advisory Committee (ACPAC), is now lobbying for the Aotea Track to be proclaimed a Great Walk, which would give it the same status as the Milford Track and the Routeburn Track.

The Aotea Track includes an old tramline track in the middle of the island, originally created to help extraction of the island's resources, which Rose and I tramped some time before the formal creation of the Aotea Track. At that time, we found a well-formed bath with hot water flowing into it which had been carved into the rock in Victorian times, apparently, at a place called the Peach Tree hot springs. The bath is at a hidden location, now somewhat overgrown and quite hard to find, just above the better-known and more accessible Kaitoke hot pools.

Making our way to Hirakimata

My friends Rose and Daniel on the path above Okiwi

In many areas the local soil seems to consist mainly of volcanic ash erupted from the now-extinct Hirakimata volcano, ash which erodes easily.

*Views to die for: looking westward from Mount Heale Hut,
and nearby, to Little Barrier Island in the distance*

I later re-did that walk by myself and visited Mount Heale Hut, which is a back-country hut with all kitchen implements, pots, pans, and even a dish brush supplied, and a view to die for. That was where I came across the *New Yorker* article I mentioned above.

MY LATEST VISIT

I spent New Year 2017/2018 on the Barrier, as Great Barrier Island is colloquially known, and I'm pleased to say it's better than ever. Some of the photos in this chapter are from my latest trip. I even swam with dolphins at Okupu (Blind Bay)! It was also great to see new community artwork.

I went to a fair at Claris, the little township next to the island's airport, which was being organised to raise money for the Aotea Family Support Group Charitable Trust. At Claris, a world champion breaks singer from New Zealand was performing. I missed out on the Great FitzRoy Mussel Fest and FitzRoy Family Festival, held at Port Fitzroy, however.

To round off, Aucklanders have long marvelled at the Barrier's starry skies, criss-crossed with clearly visible wandering satellites and streaked by meteors. A small population, lack of mains electricity, and hardly any streetlights, all help to keep the skies desert-dark even though the island isn't really all that remote.

In 2017, Great Barrier Island was awarded Dark Sky Sanctuary status by the International Dark Sky Association (ISDA), which will encourage astronomically-minded visitors. There are twelve IDA Dark Sky Reserves including one at Lake Tekapo in New Zealand, but only three Dark Sky Sanctuaries, astronomical viewing sites which are even more pristine. The three Dark Sky Sanctuaries are at Cosmic Campground in New Mexico, at the Elqui Valley in northern Chile, and now at Great Barrier Island as well.

The summer is normally the time to go to Great Barrier, because pohutukawa trees are everywhere and they blossom at Christmas. It's also the summer holidays, of course. The locals hope that Dark Sky Sanctuary status will increase winter tourism as well, since in winter the nights are longer. At that time of year, it's also possible to see the core of the Milky Way, which lies in the constellations of Scorpio and Sagittarius; whereby the Milky Way comes to look like a poached egg seen side-on rather than just a band of stars.

These constellations are most visible at mid-year and are more easily seen from the southern hemisphere than the northern because the nights at that time of year are longer in the south, it being winter downunder. The view from Great Barrier should rank with the clearest in the world, and of course one advantage of Great Barrier as a Dark Sky Sanctuary is that it is, as *National Geographic* says, only 55 miles (90 km) from the big city of Auckland.

*Eel-shaped seat at the Great Barrier Island Community
Heritage and Arts Village*

The Milky Way panorama

European Southern Observatory (ESO). CC-BY-SA 4.0
(original URL http://www.eso.org/public/images/eso0932a/)

CHAPTER FOUR

Rangitoto

A ROCKY VOLCANIC ISLAND WALK

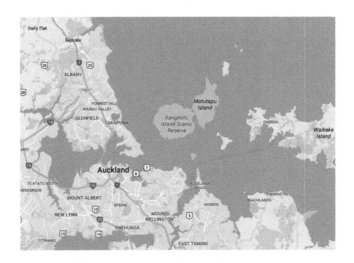

Rangitoto – a volcanic desert island in the middle of a city harbour.
(Map Data ©2017 Google)

R ANGITOTO Island is a short ferry ride from downtown Auckland city. This beautiful, rocky, island is New Zealand's youngest volcano, emerging from the sea only 600 years ago.[21] Rangitoto has since become a safe haven for wildlife, with a dedicated effort at pest eradication made by DOC before they finally declared the island to be pest-free in 2011.[22] In this natural paradise, there are a range of walks you can do either around the island or to the 260 metre (850 feet) high summit where there are great views of Auckland harbour and the Hauraki Gulf.

There are a number of baches, or cabins, on the island, which were erected by holidaymakers in a less regulated era. New construction was prohibited from 1937 onward in view of the island's wilderness character. Owners of existing baches were pressured to sign up to stringent lease conditions that presumed that the bach would be demolished at the end of the lease. Ironically, by the 1990s, the surviving baches had started to be seen as heritage buildings and they are now protected, their recent restoration even garnering an honourable mention from UNESCO!

Rangitoto summit, as seen from the coastal beginnings of the path to the summit. Note pathway, bushes and bare basalt.

Coastal areas of Rangitoto Island, with holiday bach

Clambering up from the jetty toward the bush-filled crater with its red scoria base (top right). Bare rocky basalt is abundant between the trees everywhere.

CHAPTER FIVE

Tiritiri Matangi Island

HOW WE SAVE OUR BIRDS AND REPTILES

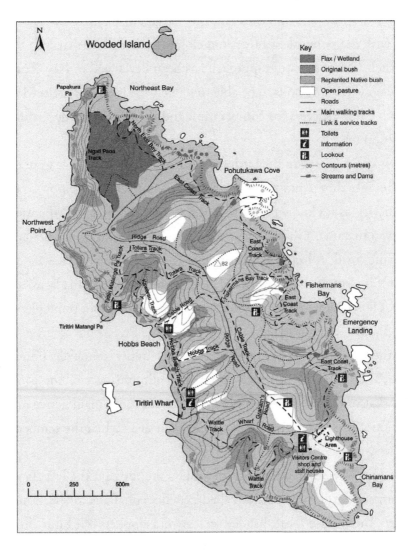

Map of Tiritiri Matangi Island. (DOC, 2017)

Tiriti Matanga is a small island in the Hauraki Gulf, 4 km off the coast north of Auckland, where I went to serve as a DOC volunteer. Tiritiri Matangi means 'tossed by the wind'. The island was farmed for many years, but in 1971 it was given to the government to become a recreation reserve and is now a nature reserve where the public can stay.[23] I was talking to people on the island and they said they originally planted sections of the island with the pohutukawa trees too close together for the trees to thrive. Since then a more scientific approach has been developed in New Zealand, and we now have the skills to be able to replant the islands. Tiritiri Matangi has been a huge success for conservation and there is also a successful kiwi population there.

I saw kiwi foraging in the bush with my red-light torch – we went out at night because they're mostly nocturnal. Apparently, there are now so many kiwi on Tiri (as it's known locally) that there are too many for the island. I also saw a tuatara on the beach. This is really something as the tuatara is a true living fossil. A lizard-like creature with spines on its back – its Māori name means 'spiny one' – the tuatara looks a lot like an iguana lizard at first glance. Like the iguana, it has golden eyes and a vertical slit pupil like a cat, an adaptation to night living.

All the same, the tuatara and the iguana are almost completely unrelated. Indeed, the tuatara is not even a lizard at all, and part of the proof of that is that, unlike 'normal' reptiles, the tuatara can remain active in cold conditions. The tuatara is able to move about even when the temperature is as low as five degrees Celsius!

The two New Zealand species of tuatara are, in fact, the last survivors of an ancient group of reptiles called rynchocephalians, or beak-headed reptiles. The phrase 'beak-headed' refers to a hooked bill built into the structure of the skull of the tuatara and its extinct relatives, along with bony spikes that resemble teeth although they are not true teeth. The effect is to produce a skull that looks like the skull of a small predatory mammal like a weasel in some ways, with pronounced fangs at the front, except that the effect of fangs is produced by the hook-like projection at the very front of the tuatara skull.[24]

And so, the tuatara makes its living as a small, night-stalking predator capable of taking a young bird as yet unable to fly, or even a rat, in addition to the lizards, insects, worms and eggs that are the mainstay of its diet.[25]

Like the kiwi, the tuatara is a 'wannabe mammal', a creature which is not a mammal but which pursues a way of life that, in other parts of the world, would be carried on by mammals. If the snuffling kiwi is a bird that thinks it is a hedgehog, as the saying goes, then by the same token, the tuatara is a reptile that thinks it is a weasel.

In New Zealand, there are also certain small darting birds that, in the same sense, think they are mice. Even the birds that were more like 'normal' birds were often poor fliers and nested on the ground. All of these creatures evolved in the partial or complete absence of mammals and survived in the absence of mammals, save for a couple of species of bat.

Like the kiwi and other New Zealand 'wannabe mammals', and ground-nesting birds, the tuatara thrived only so long as mammalian rivals and/or predators did not make it to these shores. The very cold-bloodedness of the tuatara limited its appetite and the rate at which it was liable to breed. Not so the honest-to-goodness mammalian predator, the existence of which soon upset New Zealand's rather sedate ecological applecart.

That is why pest-controlled island sanctuaries like Tiritiri Matangi are so important in the story of New Zealand conservation. For the stories of the kiwi and the tuatara could be repeated, with variations, for many New

Zealand species that now depend on offshore islands as refuges from the rat, the stoat, the cat or the dog.

It was interesting talking to the other volunteers when I was on Tiritiri Matangi. Two of them had helped to fund the bird research themselves, and the others came from zoos in Australia and the Auckland Zoo, so the birds were very well cared for.

One particularly rare bird on the island is the kōkako, which I was fortunate enough to see, and to hear their haunting call.

The island also holds takahē of which there aren't many left, though they have been successfully bred. It's sad that we've lost the bellbird (korimako) in Auckland and the Waitakere Ranges, as they're almost completely absent on the mainland north of Hamilton.[26] They're not even reintroducing them. However, thankfully there are a lot on Tiritiri. There were also many stitch birds (hihi) and kākāriki, a term that refers to two closely related species of parakeet.

The lighthouse on Tiritiri Matangi is interesting. Of the usual round-pillar appearance, it was built from cast iron in 1864 and is still in operation. Until 1947 it was painted red, appearing dark in old photographs, and there is some talk of painting it red once more.

As a DOC volunteer, my duties included dissolving sugar in water to feed the bellbirds and the tūī and I was just surrounded by all these birds coming to get the food. As the bush has matured now they don't rely on the sugar feed so much. A lot of visitors come from Auckland and there are plenty of volunteers who show them around and talk about the island's history. The volunteers are very proud of their work, and one lady, an old volunteer, even told me that it was *her* island and we shouldn't trust the government with it, as they were the ones who had let the bird population dwindle until there was almost none left. They couldn't look after the birds, and they couldn't look after the island. She was very territorial – but with a beautiful, natural place like Tiritiri Matangi Island, I can almost see why.

Takahē.

Photographed by Ashleigh Thompson on Tiritiri Matangi Island. CC-BY-2.0. https://upload.wikimedia.org/ wikipedia/ commons/7/74/ Porphyrio_ hochstetteri_-Tiritiri_ Matangi_Island-8b-3c.jpg

Signal Tower (below), beside the Lighthouse

Tiritiri Matangi Lighthouse and another view of the Signal Tower (right).

Detail from photograph by 'Avenue', CC-BY-SA 3.0. https://upload.wikimedia.org/ wikipedia/commons/8/80/ Tiritri_Matangi_lighthouse_and_macrocarpa_tree.jpg

Tieke or Saddleback.

Photographed on Tiritiri Matangi Island by Duncan Wright.

CC-BY-SA 3.0.

https://upload.wikimedia.org/ wikipedia/ commons/0/0d/ Saddleback_tiritiri.jpg

Kōkako.

Photographed by Doug Mak at Pukaha Mount Bruce National Wildlife Centre, Masterton. Originally posted to Flickr as Kokako, CC-BY-SA 2.0.

https://commons.wikimedia.org/ wiki/File:K%C5%8Dkako.jpg

CHAPTER SIX

Auckland's Undiscovered Secrets

L OCATED just a 30-minute drive west from downtown Auckland, the Hillary Trail is one of Auckland's best-kept secrets. It's too well kept a secret, really, as many Aucklanders have yet to experience it. Like me, they may take a long time to find it. Some Aucklanders, however, like the fact that it *is* a secret.

Named after New Zealand's most famous explorer, Sir Edmund Hillary, whom a friend of mine has kindly sketched for this book (at left), the track  takes you through the Waitakere Ranges Regional Park, along wild coastline, past countless waterfalls, and through ancient bush.[27] A massive possum control effort has managed to make the park 98% possum free, so the bush is really lush and healthy. There is a local organisation named Ark in the Park, which, as well as keeping out predators, looks after the area by reintroducing rare native birds such as kōkako into parts of it.[28]

Looking to explore the full length of the trail, some friends and I had an itinerary of four days and three nights, leaving from the Auckland suburb of Titirangi and heading through the Arataki Visitor Centre to tramp to the Karamatura Valley Campsite just west of the coastal settlement of Huia.

I've show a couple of satellite images on which the Hillary Trail is marked up along with a mid-point access route from the Swanson Railway Station. I should emphasise that this is no substitute for a proper trail map, as the

Waitakere Ranges are covered by a dense network of trails and it is easy to get lost. For instance, the railway-station access route shown as a broken line is not a single trail but is in fact made up, from east to west, of Tram Valley Road followed by sections of the Swanson Pipeline Track, the Peripatus Track, the Anderson Track, the Auckland City Walk, the Upper Kauri Track,

The Hillary Trail and its Environs.
(Based on NASA Earth Observatory jpeg image Auckland_17_2002239)

the Long Road Track and the Smyth Ridge Track. So, you can see it really does pay to get a proper map and leaflet before exploring this area!

Titirangi is well worth stopping in for a cup of coffee. On the edge of the city, this suburb is already well into the primordial bush of the west coast, with glimpses of the Manukau Harbour and its heads to be seen from some of the cafes in buildings in the Titirangi village, buildings such as Lopdell House, an Art Deco structure that opened in 1930 as the Hotel Titirangi, and eventually became an arts centre.

In front of Lopdell House is a statue of a noted early Auckland environmentalist and water engineer, Henry Atkinson. Not the same as the colonial New Zealand premier Harry Atkinson, Henry Atkinson was, rather, Auckland's nearest equivalent to Los Angeles's Walter Mulholland.

Henry Atkinson acquired much of the wilderness west of Auckland on his own account while laying out grand public waterworks in the same area, and then donated the surplus bush to Auckland for conservation purposes.[29]

Up a steep hill and never served by tram in the days when most people used trams to get around, Titirangi was once a notable artists' retreat – a bit like Heidelberg in Melbourne, for instance – and still has some of that vibe, as well as several rather Bohemian cafés, grand scenic views of the Manukau Harbour and a feeling of being on the edge of the bush: altogether, an ideal place to begin a nature ramble.

From Karamatura, we headed to Whatipu, then faced a tramp of slightly over ten kilometres from Whatipu to the Karekare Tunnel Point Campground, before heading to Anawhata and on through to come out at Swanson, though it is also possible to finish at Muriwai. You can get to the beginning of the track at the visitor centre by bus. Or if you are in group, leave one car where you start and another car at the end.

The tunnel at Tunnel Point, Karekare, also known as the Pararaha Tunnel, was drilled more than a hundred years ago for the transportation of kauri logs along the coast from Piha to Whatipu by means of an industrial tram line known as the Piha Tramway, which ran all the way from Anawhata to Whatipu via Piha, where a sawmill was located.

The Piha Tramway operated between the dates of 1906 and 1921 approximately, a short interval in retrospect. Native timber, principally kauri, had been logged in the Waitakeres since 1836, and the coastal stands were the last and hardest to get at. They didn't last long once modern technology, modern by the standards of 1906 at any rate, was applied to getting them.[30]

There is an old rusting boiler next to the tunnel today, perhaps of the very engine shown in the photo on the previous page.

Going back further in time, if you've seen the Victorian period drama *The Piano*, starring Holly Hunter, Anna Paquin and Harvey Keitel, this is the very place where most of it was filmed, and set. Auckland's wild west, battered by sea winds and spray from the Tasman Seal and dominated by hills and dunes covered in tough, leathery plants, is less touristy but at the same time more primeval than the east coast of the Auckland region, which is quite sheltered and faces the Pacific.

Phrases used to describe sections of the eastern, Pacific coast of the Auckland region, such as 'Hibiscus Coast', suggest an incipient Gold Coast syndrome of touristy over-development and retiree communities. On the other hand, only hardy souls visit the wild West Coast of the Auckland region, and there is not much development: surprisingly little when you consider that there is a big city only an hour away.

There is plenty of up and down-hill on the Hillary Trail, including steep sections that would be challenging with a heavy backpack, as well as a few shallow steams to cross. Furthermore, the stretches of tramping between stops are long and arduous, especially the last day from Craw Campsite to Muriwai, which traverses a whopping 27 km in eleven or twelve hours.

Under each section of the track in the descriptions below, I have included day walks which can be done separately from the entire trail. If you want to

The mouth of the Pararaha Tunnel on the Piha tram line, with a group of workers standing beside the logging locomotive "Sandfly". Piha sawmill manager Mr H. P. Knutzen is seated on the front of the engine.

Photographed by Albert Percy Godber between 1915 and 1916. A. P. Godber collection, Alexander Turnbull Library (Wellington), reference APG-0826-1/2-G.

make your trek longer, you can always spend more time in each area. The trail is mostly on tramping tracks which are rough, uneven, and muddy in places. While the Hillary Trail can be tramped in winter, if the weather has been wet the mud can be right up to your knees or higher.

It is easy to get food along the way. Even at Karamatura you can access a shop at Huia only 15 minutes from the campground by car. Between Karekare and Anawhata you can get food at Piha, as we did; and at Muriwai you can also drop into a store. This will slow you down, but as you will need to bring less food it will keep your backpacks lighter.

ARATAKI VISITOR CENTRE TO KARAMATURA VALLEY CAMPSITE

From the visitor centre, the trail starts by descending into the Nihotupu Valley before turning right onto Pipeline Track, which leads onto Lower Nihotupu Dam Road before joining the Hamilton Track. Entering the interior of the Waitakere Ranges, the trail reaches Crusher Pipe Track, and then takes Smiths Road over the Lower Huia Reservoir onto Huia Dam Road, which holds the most recently-built water supply dam in the Ranges.[31] At the bridge on the edge of Huia Bay, the Hillary Trail continues along the shoreline to the Karamatura Valley.

At the Karamatura Valley carpark there is a very striking pou whenua or 'land post' Land posts can be as tall as totem poles from British Columbia or Alaska and are used to tell ancestral stories in a similar way, though the one at Karamatura is rather stubby. Carved by members of the Te Kawarau a Maki people, it depicts a shark, reminding everyone that Te Kawarau a Maki have long caught sharks in this area; and on top, two fugitive lovers hiding behind a local waterfall, where they were temporarily deafened by

Top: *Beach at Huia. The Awhitu Peninsula is in the far distance, the north head of the Manukau Harbour at right.*

Right: *Pou Whenua depicting a waterfall sheltering fugitive lovers, on top of a depiction of a shark, at the Karamatura Valley Carpark*

Bottom: *Manukau Heads, from north head hills near Huia*

Karamatura

the noise. As such, Karamatura has also been called Kaingamaturi: which means 'dwelling place of the deaf'.

KARAMATURA TO WHATIPU

The second leg of the tramp takes walkers out to the Manukau Harbour along the high Omanawanui Track to the historic milling settlement of Whatipu. The Omanawanui Track has really spectacular views of the Manukau Heads and the Awhitu Peninsula.

Other things being equal, the Awhitu Peninsula might have been the logical place to have founded the city of Auckland, facing westward to Australia and closer to the fertile farmlands of the Waikato than Auckland itself. However, the entrance to Manukau Harbour is not particularly navigable. A huge mass of sand slowly migrating northward on the seaward side chokes the entrance, and forms the great seaward land-mass of Whatipu just to the north of the Manukau Heads.

Partly for that reason, the city of Auckland which had been founded on the isthmus to the east in 1840 developed around the rival Waitematā Harbour which is entered from the east, even by ships sailing from Australia. In February 1863, a treacherous sand-bar off the Manukau Heads caused the sinking, with great loss of life, of HMS Orpheus, flagship of the Royal Navy's Australian squadron: a disaster that hammered the final nail into the coffin of any civic ambitions that might have been entertained for the Awhitu Peninsula and the Manukau Harbour at that time.

The Awhitu Peninsula remains undeveloped to this day: in the words of a recent article the peninsula is Auckland's 'best-kept secret', even more so than the Hillary Trail to the north of the heads in other words; though given that it is mostly in farmland, the Awhitu Peninsula is not as exotic or bush-clad as the terrain through which the Hillary Trail runs.[32]

Manukau Heads as seen from the Omanawanui Track

WHATIPU TO KAREKARE

At Whatipu, the great sand mass that is slowly migrating up the coast projects out into the ocean for some kilometres, forming an area of flat and sandy landscape to the west of the rocky massif of the Waitakeres. After a night at Whatipu, walkers traverse the Whatipu Scientific Reserve through sand dunes and around gorgeous dune-impounded lakes teeming with wildlife, through the Pararaha Gorge – another old milling site – if they so desire (see below), to Karekare beach. Both Karekare and the next beach along the trail, Piha, are two of New Zealand's most iconic stretches of coastline. This is especially true for Piha with its raging surf.

The route between Whatipu and Karekare is a complete loop or circuit in its own right; though anyone doing the Hillary Trail one way will generally do Whatipu to Karekare, or vice versa, one way as well.

Whatipu as seen from the Omanawanui Track

It is possible to walk along the beach from Whatipu to Karekare, and there are also several alternative inland routes for all or part of the way. The toughest is the Pararaha Gorge route, of which I have some photos below. This gorge should only be approached by experienced trampers, even as a day-walk destination.

Whapitu-to-Karekare Coast

Whapitu-to-Karekare Coast

Whapitu-to-Karekare Coast

Whapitu-to-Karekare
Coast

Looking south from the Watchman (hill) at Karekare, over the Karekare Stream, past Karekare Point and Panatahi Island to ward Whatipu

*Whatipu to Karekare-Paraha
Stream Route*

Whatipu to Karekare-Pararaha Stream Route. The sunless Pararaha Gorge, above.

Picture at the right shows pool with ice on top, small bubbles visible top right of this photo!

Very unusual near Auckland!

*Whatipu to Karekare-Pararaha
Stream Route*

*Whatipu to
Karekare-Pararaha
Stream Route*

*Karekare
Contrasts*

97

Panatahi Island, off Karekare Point, the last headland normally passable at high tide for the northbound coastal rambler

Farley Point at the north end of Karekare Beach is normally impassable at high tide

The dramatic Mercer Bay north of Farley Point: Te Ahua Point is shown in this view

KAREKARE TO ANAWHATA VIA PIHA, WITH DETOURS

Only four hours approximately, covering a distance of eleven kilometres, the Karekare to Piha stretch of the tramp can easily be done within a day. From Piha Beach it is a bit less than five kilometres through to Anawhata Farm, and a bit further on down to Anawhata Beach.

Overlooked by hilltop roads and by Lion Rock on the beach itself, Piha is the best-known and most developed of the Auckland West Coast beaches, with cafés and a small township. Even so it is still very wild by most people's standards, and somewhat dangerous for swimming as well, like all the West Coast beaches.

From Piha it is possible to hike up inland tracks to the Anawhata Road and the Piha Road, notably up the Piha Valley Track along the Piha Stream. This is a detour from the official Hillary Trail, but one well worth making. The gnarly Piha Gorge, similar to the Pararaha Gorge, is optional, and is suitable for experienced trampers only even as a day-walk just up to the gorge and back.

Anawahata Beach is *also* a detour from the official Hillary Trail, which runs well inland past Anawhata Beach and over the Anawhata Stream via the Kuataika Track. Again, it, too, is a detour well worth making! Well-prepared groups can exit the beach to the Kuataika Track via the Anawhata Stream.

Piha Beach and township with Lion Rock

Piha blowholes, sea cave and hilltop view

The Piha Stream

The Piha Gorge and evirons, including example of unusual-looking 'basket fungus'

Piha

North Piha

Anawahata Farm,
above the beach

Could almost
touch the sky
up here

*Scenes on the Kuataika
Track, which bypasses
Anawhata Beach*

Anawhata Beach

Anawhata

Anawhata

Anawhata

Anawhata

Anawhata Stream – another gnarly and old-fashioned way in from the coast, but at least we weren't carrying a piano!

ANAWHATA TO BETHELLS BEACH

From Anawhata, it is twelve and a half kilometres to Te Henga (Bethells Beach), where the beautiful Lake Wainamu and some giant sand dunes crowning another beach with impressive surf are to be found. When we

Anawhata Stream

tramped the trail, we ended up going through Te Henga/Bethells, which is a beach I've had a long association with. The beach has a cave known as the Ballroom, where I have once been to a gathering of witches, or Wiccans. We didn't go all the way to Muriwai, instead walking to Scenic Drive where our car was parked. And that's where we finished.

Lake Wainamu from the south end, beach dunes at the north end

Lake Wainamu from the north end

People hiking toward Lake Wainamu from Bethells Beach

113

Scenes on the way from Anawhata to Lake Wainamu

Nature near
Lake Wainamu

Bethells Beach

Bethells Beach

117

Bethells Beach

Bethells Beach

BETHELLS BEACH TO MURIWAI

The last section of the Hillary Trail proceeds along an exposed cliff-top walkway, the Te Henga Walkway, for five or six hours before finishing at Muriwai Beach.

This walk can also be done as part of a local loop by linking up with the more inland Goldies Bush Track back to Bethells Beach.

Te Henga Walkway, northward from Bethells Beach to Muriwai

Te Henga Walkway Landscapes

Te Henga Walkway – with Kevin Williams, Nicki Botica Williams and their friend Paul Borich in the lower photograph

Goldies Bush Track – much moister and more subtropical than Te Henga walkway Note the lurid 'flower fungus', a relative of the White Basket

Goldies Bush Track

Muriwai

Muriwai

OUR JOURNEY ALONG THE HILLARY TRAIL

We started out at the Arataki Visitor Centre on Scenic Drive and spent the first night tenting in Huia near the Karamatura Valley. However, it was Whatipu where our walk truly began, parking one car there and leaving another car at the other end. We then made our way around the rocks at Whatipu, beginning our great coastal walk.

From Whatipu we tried to make our way around to Karekare Peninsula. That was very hard because the person who said he knew the way really had no idea and we ended up stuck in the mud. This is a recognised hazard with the Whatipu dunelands, especially if it has been wet lately. The temptation is to stick close to the cliffs as they are furthest inland and form the most direct route north-south, but it is precisely there that you are likely to end up chest-deep in something wet. We could have taken the Valley Trail or have stayed at the Pararaha Valley, or simply stuck to the beach, but chose not to and instead got wet in swampy dunelands.

I'd done Pararaha Valley before with Stephen French from the Feet First meetup group (for reasons I have explained in *A Maverick Traveller*, in recent years, people have tended to go on meetup group hikes as opposed to joining the older tramping clubs). While it would have been a good idea to do it again with this group, in the end we found our way out of the dunelands – having run out of clean drinking water, another hazard – and finally made it back to somewhere a bit less wild. We stayed at the Tunnel Point camp ground, a busy camping spot with a toilet and quite a number of people. However, to our dismay it was also short of drinking water and we had to get water out of a smelly stream. Luckily, we were told the best place to find fresh water soon after.

As I mentioned above, there is a history of logging in this area, starting in the early 1900s when a lot of virgin kauri was cleared, leaving the hillsides bare and empty. However, new kauri are starting to grow back, albeit very slowly, for a hundred years is not long in the life of the kauri. The kauri is a classic old-growth forest species, and capable of growing to an enormous size, not just in terms of height but also in terms of girth. It would be said that each big kauri tree contained the timber for two average-sized houses; Tāne Mahuta contains enough for about four. Quite often in back-country spots you will come across a section the stump of some big old kauri cut down a hundred or so years ago, with various dates indicated on the rings: Columbus, the Battle of Hastings, maybe even Jesus perhaps. But young and slender kauri were also valued for the way that they grew straight and true; in the days of sail, they were considered ideal for ship's masts.

A tramline was built along Auckland's west coast for 66 kilometres to service the logging industry,[33] with a tunnel cutting through the hill at Karekare so that the tramline did not have to go around the point.

Eventually, we got to the Karekare tunnel and then visited Karekare Falls and saw an amazing sunset from there.

From Karekare we had hoped to get to Anawhata beach, which made for a long day walking along Coman's track, along Piha Road, Te Ahu Ahu Rd, Log Race Rd, and down to Piha Beach. It was very hilly and not an easy walk at all. We hit a café in Piha and were quite hungry because we'd only had tramping food, and Paul, one of our group, was able to buy a much-needed hat to keep the sun off. After lunch, we made our way to Anawhata beach, a beautiful black sand beach. There's an alternative side walk up to Anawhata beach which includes White's beach.

Like Whatipu, Anawhata is only accessible on foot, making it one of the quietest of Auckland's west coast beaches. There's a carpark at the end of the road and the public can walk either to the waterfall or to the beach, which takes about ten minutes.

My friends and I camped out along the Hillary Trail. But there are many private- and council-owned huts and campgrounds along the walk which can be booked in advance and paid in full on arrival. Otherwise, the Hillary Trail really is a beautiful, wild trail and a great opportunity to get out of the busy city. I think it's something all Aucklanders, if not all New Zealanders, should walk at least once in their lives.

As you can see from the photographs, there are probably few places on earth, least of all beaches, that are so primordial and quite often deserted, and yet so close to a big city.

Update: An increasing number of tracks have been closed, and a rāhui or traditional ban proclaimed, to try and prevent the spread of kauri dieback disease in the Waitakere ranges. Visitors to the Waitakeres should make themselves familiar with this issue. (Hopefully, a remedy will soon be found.)

CHAPTER SEVEN
The Pinnacles
HUNDREDS OF STEPS IN ROCK

The Pinnacles Hut is top centre in this area of the lower Coromandel Peninsula, the Firth of Thames left. Map data ©2017 Google.

Y mother fell in love with the Kauaeranga Valley near Thames on the Coromandel Peninsula, and decided to move there from Hastings in 1980. I proceeded to do walks in the area right through the '80s and into the '90s. I tramped the Pinnacles Walk, also called the Kauaeranga Kauri Trail, for the first time in the 1980s and have since done it about ten times. At the bottom of my parents' property an old bush tramway runs past, which was used to transport the kauri out to Thames in the logging days, where it was processed and taken by barge to Auckland. Because of the rugged terrain, it was difficult to get the massive logs out from the more remote areas, so they used to dam the rivers and then release the dams to let the kauri float down to where it could be collected by the tramway.[34] You can still see the remains of some of these kauri dams today.

The Pinnacles walk is highly rated as something of a must-do for New Zealanders, and well worth it for tourists as well. The track up to the Pinnacles is not especially difficult for a fit person, as it was carved into the form of a staircase (in the steeper sections) so that kauri loggers, miners, and kauri gum diggers, excavating the ground for unfossilised resin, could get pack horses up and down.[35]

I love doing the Pinnacles Walk because it's over varied terrain. You start at the end of the Kauaeranga Valley Road and head over a swing bridge across the Kauaeranga River, where there are lovely black rocks. The regenerating bush has a lot of new kauri, which is really satisfying. From the junction, you follow the Webb Creek Track to Hydro Camp, walking towards the summit up steps which were cut into the rock by the loggers to make it easier for their packhorses to get through.[36] The rock is granite-like and very similar to the rock on Great Barrier Island.

The Pinnacles summit is only 759 metres high, so it's not classified as subalpine like a couple of the other bush rambles I discuss below, Pirongia and Waikaremoana, which are a bit higher.

Still, the track is quite steep in places, above all on the Pinnacles themselves. Just below the summit, the Pinnacles are fitted with climbing ladders. Obviously, this last section is no longer part of the pack-horse route.

The Pinnacles Hut, which is at the foot of the Pinnacles proper, and as such located on the pack-horse part of the route, sleeps 80 people. Even so, it is recommended to book ahead in view of the popularity and accessibility of this walk. Many people of all ages walk up to the hut all the time, even if they have no intention of venturing up the ladders all the way to the top of the Pinnacles.

The Kauaeranga Valley is a beautiful place. All the same, it has seen a lot of extractive industry. In addition to logging, mining used to be a mainstay of the local economy, and gold mining has started up again lately. Both my family and many of the other residents in the area want it to stop because it's very polluting to the natural landscape of the valley.

Climbing up to the Pinnacles via the old pack-horse route created by miners, kauri loggers and kauri gum diggers in the early 1900s

133

Views from higher up. The Pinnacles Hut is in the centre, as seen from the Pinnacles themselves. A view out over the Pacific Ocean is at bottom

CHAPTER EIGHT

Mount Te Aroha

A REASON FOR NO MORE MINING

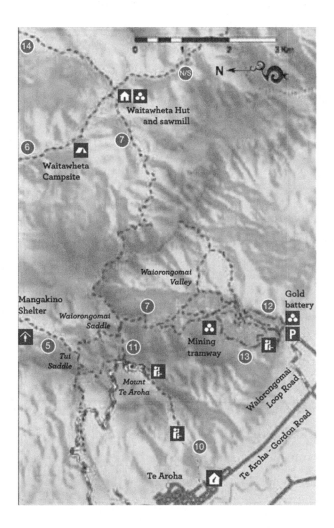

Te Aroha and Wairongomai Tracks. From *Kaimai to Coast / Walks and Tramps* (brochure), Department of Conservation, Tauranga, March 2014

I've done Mount Te Aroha twice. At 952 metres, it's the highest peak in the Kaimai-Mamaku Range, and is located 45 minutes north of Hamilton.[37] Although the climb isn't challenging and it takes only three hours to reach the summit, I once did it with a friend who wasn't very fit. He hadn't done any tramping at all and we were quite worried for him before someone finally took his backpack to ease his load.

A highlight of Mount Te Aroha is the group of hot springs at the foot of the mountain. These springs have been used for hundreds of years for their healing properties. In the late 1800s the land was gifted to New Zealand by the Māori chief Mokena Hou to be used as a public health resort, and has remained a popular spot for bathers ever since.[38] There are many other hot springs in the Waikato area and the North Island, and some in the South Island as well.

Despite its natural beauty, Mount Te Aroha itself has been polluted by gold mining in the past and there is evidence of this that you can see on one slope. This unfortunate reality was brought about by a huge gold rush to the area in the late 1880s leading to a massive boom in the nearby township of Te Aroha. However, while there was little gold to be found and the disappointed miners soon left town, they certainly left their mark on the area. Much of the vegetation on the mountain hides rotting mine shafts and tunnels, a danger that DOC attempts to oversee by telling visitors to keep to marked tracks and not to enter tunnels.[39] Much of the mountain doesn't have any bush and in the wet it's miserable, especially when a thick fog closes in and wipes out the scenic views of the Waikato and Bay of Plenty – it's most definitely one to do in the summer!

Typical Mount Te Aroha terrain

*View from the top
of Mount Te Aroha,
with the Pacific
Ocean in the distance*

*Tracks on Mount
Te Aroha*

CHAPTER NINE

Pirongia

PRETTY SUBALPINE CLIMB IN BOG

Pirongia, southwest of Hamilton
Map Data ©2017 Google

PIRONGIA is a subalpine mountain with beautiful granite rock faces, which, at 959 metres high, easily has the highest peak in the Waikato region. At only 25 kilometres southeast of Hamilton, the mountain is also the largest remaining area of native forest close to the city.[40]

Although there are several routes to the summit, when I tramped it we took the 18.5-kilometre-long Bell Track to the top, heading past the Kaniwhaniwha Caves and along a ridge to the Cone, which is the second-highest point on Mt Pirongia. The Bell Track is very much up and down, as is the form of Mount Pirongia itself, so you will end up climbing a lot more than 959 metres in total: be warned! From the Cone, we carried on to the Pahautea Hut, where it's another thirty minutes to the summit. The track itself forms part of the Waikato section of Te Araroa, meaning 'The Long Path', a trail that takes you the length of New Zealand all the way from Cape Reinga to Bluff.

I tramped Pirongia in the summer and found that despite the heat, it was very muddy at the top. There were three of us in the tramping party, one of whom was an unfit, overweight woman who carried four litres of water and refused to lighten her pack. Consequently, walking the Bell Track took us ten hours. I was very sorry for the guy with her because he ended up carrying some of the food from her pack, as well as having to help her up to the top. Then she wanted to pitch her tent in the middle of nowhere at nine p.m. Thankfully, I had saved them the last two beds in the Pahautea Hut, which the poor guy was very happy about. She also wanted to trek into the night, but I refused because the track was a very marshy, peaty type of soil and we could have easily become stuck or at least lost a hiking boot or two in the dark.

The peaty soil grows beautiful subalpine ferns, and for anyone who is interested in ferns, Pirongia is a special treat.

Pirongia

CHAPTER TEN

White Island

AN ISLAND WITH GEYSERS AND A LIVE VOLCANO

White Island, indicated by a circle, in the Bay of Plenty.
(Map Data ©2017 Google)

L OCATED eighty minutes off the coast from Whakatane in the Bay of Plenty, the remote White Island is New Zealand's most active volcano, with a minor eruption last occurring in April 2016.[41] Despite this, many visitors are drawn to the island for its natural beauty and geothermal activity, as well as the abundance of marine life near the island, tours to which are run by White Island Tours Ltd.

The island contains large amounts of sulphur which in the past was mined for making acid, fertiliser, and industrial chemicals. Sulphurous minerals, dissolved in groundwater, also run into the sea off White Island in the form of a natural chemical plume which is toxic near the island but which has a fertilising effect on the sea life as it becomes diluted, further out.

My friends Kevin and Nicki Williams, who have provided many of the photographs in this book, have also shared some wonderful photos of White Island that illustrate this chapter. Kevin had an uncle who died while working on the island as a miner. More specifically his grandfather's brother, John Williams, was a fireman – which in steam-engineering parlance meant someone responsible for operating a boiler – who was killed one day when the boiler he was tending blew up.

In addition to accidents resulting from the lax industrial safety standards of the era, all the workers on the island were killed during an eruption on 10 September 1914. The only survivor was the camp cat, Peter the Great, who had found a good place to hide till it was all over (Whence, the legend that a cat has nine lives. When something terrible happens, cats can take refuge more easily than a human and are often smart enough to figure out when they need to do so).

Sulphur mining was abandoned after the calamity of 1914. Mining began again in the 1920s but was permanently given up in the 1930s as prices fell, most probably to everyone's relief I suspect. White Island was abandoned thereafter to the birds, to the fish, and to short-stay tourists prepared to accept the modest risk of visiting the shaky and sulphurous island for just a few hours.

White Island, with crater and boiling mud pools

*White Island
volcanic landscapes,
a contrast of yellow
sulphur and blue
sky*

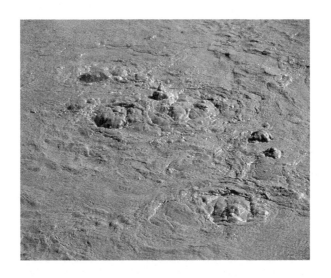

Boiling mud and steam

CHAPTER ELEVEN

Waikaremoana

STEEPED IN MĀORITANGA

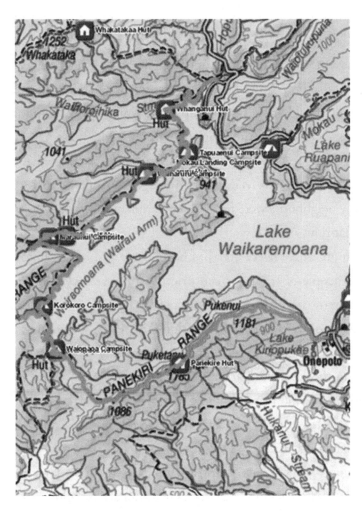

The Path trampers take around the un-roaded side of Lake Waikaremoana. Source: DOC Website

As a child I gained a strong connection to Lake Waikare-moana, the lake of rippling waters, which is located in the Māori stewardship area of Te Urewera (formerly Te Urewera National Park). Since Waikaremoana is only a few hours north of Hastings, my family used to camp out at the lake every Christmas holidays from when I was six years old until I was about sixteen. I tramped the area extensively in 1995 and 1998 and redid it in 2008 and in 2012 – I always seem to keep coming back there.

The area is home to the Ngāi Tūhoe people, a local Māori tribe, and even as a young child I recognised their strong presence in the area. I remember that when we would drive into Murupara we would always being amazed at how everyone working in the shop spoke Māori, which I loved. The native language is very strong here, and they still speak in the Tūhoe dialect to this day. I spoke fairly fluent Māori from the age of about 12 to 18 years old because my neighbours were from Whanganui and spoke Māori often, but I've lost that now.

The remote Te Urewera area has been home to Ngāi Tūhoe, meaning the Tūhoe people or tribe, for centuries; and it was they who named the lake 'Waikaremoana', which means 'sea of the rippling waters'. Tūhoe were one of the Māori tribes who did not sign the Treaty of Waitangi, and have a strong history of seeking independence from the Crown. In the process of claiming the land back from government ownership they have held many protests, including stealing the million-New-Zealand-dollar Urewera Tryptych, painted in 1975 by Colin McCahon, from the visitor centre near Waikaremoana in 1997.

McCahon, a Pākehā artist and tortured alcoholic in later years – an inhabitant of Titirangi in the days when it was an artists' colony – had felt an urge to channel Māori spirituality, expressed in words in the Māori language that he painted over the surface of ever more abstract-looking landscapes.

McCahon's works were regularly derided by philistines who thought that art should look pretty. Among those of a more liberal temperament, McCahon's work was regarded as highly innovative and progressive. Even so, it could be said that it appropriated Māori themes without appropriate cultural permission.

And so, the painting's text, and its presentation to the visitor centre by McCahon, caused controversy amongst the Tūhoe people since it was seen as a disrespectful appropriation of Māori culture. Even so, the painting was regarded as an important artwork. One of the painting's abductors, an activist named Te Kaha, said they took it to 'show [the government] what it feels like to have your treasures taken off you forcibly'.[42]

The culturally controversial painting was eventually returned after the intercession of a prodigiously wealthy Auckland patron of the arts, Jenny Gibbs, who was driven to a secret location by Māori rebels with her hands over her eyes; surely a lot more exciting than the average wine and cheese evening at the Auckland City Art Gallery. When the dust settled, the painting was now estimated to be worth two million New Zealand dollars, the whole business having given it considerable publicity.[43] Not, of course, that it was ever actually for sale as everyone understood that whatever the politics of the affair, we were talking about a cultural treasure and questions of mutual respect.

A short hike from the visitor centre takes you to the nearby Lake Waikareiti, meaning the little rippling waters. It's a great place to for kayaking, and if you kayak out to Rahui Island and climb the metal ladder, you can see the beautiful Lake Tamaiti o Waikaremoana, or little child of the rippling waters – a lake within a lake!

My friends and I had stopped by Tamaiti o Waikaremoana to camp out, and another tramper on the island came up to me and gave me some trout so I gave him a bag of marshmallows and some biscuits in return. He told me that he was fishing and hunting, and was planning to take some of the extra venison he'd caught to another island on the lake where local Māori where camping. He said that the Tūhoe had a tradition that if they turn up three weeks before Christmas and name their campground by staking their rights to Māori land, they can stay there for free.

In my Nissan van I had a big *Tino Rangatiratanga* flag which I put on the back of the van. This Māori flag is based on the principles of *Tino Rangatiratanga*, which refers to their absolute sovereignty over their own lives and land – something I fully believe in. However, at Lake Waikaremoana, some locals came up to me and asked why white people were flying that flag, and they didn't understand when I told them I liked the design and agreed with their principles.

I tramped the Waikaremoana Track, which leads around the lake. One of the few New Zealand Great Walks in the North Island, Waikaremoana is a subalpine area even though it only elevates to 1,180 metres at the highest point of the track which cuts its way through the thick bush surrounding the lake. As I mention in *A Maverick Traveller*, New Zealand has an incredibly low treeline for its latitudes, at only 1,000 to 1,500 metres in most areas. The reasons for this include an absence of inland continental heating, since most places are close to the sea; wild marine weather, which stunts growth on exposed tops; and the fact that much New Zealand vegetation is descended from evergreen tropical types which cannot handle extreme cold and deep frosts.

Thus, you have the odd experience of transitioning from a lush environment that looks like tropical jungle near sea level, via a progressively more stunted 'goblin forest' or cloud forest of the kind that might be found several thousand metres up in the tropics, to exposed and freezing tundra resembling the top of Mount Kilimanjaro or the remotest parts of Iceland but at perhaps only a thousand metres above sea level, or considerably less on Stewart Island. This is something that gets a lot of unwary trampers and tourists into trouble.

The Lake Waikaremoana track reminded me of Mount Pirongia in the Waikato area, as they both have cabbage trees and Dicksonia ferns. These beautiful native trees can be seen all over New Zealand in areas ranging from home gardens to wild bush. The cabbage tree tends to prefer wide open spaces such as farms where it gets full sunlight. The area around Lake Waikaremoana is also home to many other native New Zealand plants and birds.

I was tramping around the lake with four people I didn't know in a walk organised by a group called Auckland Outdoors. Although I enjoyed their company, two of them drank heavily during the tramp, which was to cause disagreements later in the tramp. I stayed back a little from the group, not wanting to be caught up in any unruly behaviour but just enjoy the peaceful environment of the track.

We took the normal 8.8-km route from Onepoto to Panekire Hut, which takes about five hours according to DOC and is the only major uphill part of the walk. However, the views from the top of Panekire make it worth it – on a good day you can see right out to Wairoa and Gisborne. We had a good day tramping, and though we didn't see a single DOC ranger in the area, there was plenty of pest control around, which was good, as the native bird population there often suffers from predators such as rats and stoats. There were a lot of hunters around as well, no doubt hoping to cull some of the deer in the area.

I knew this part of the walk well, as I had tramped to Panekire Hut once before in 1995. While the hut hadn't changed much, the company there

*Why I keep coming back to Lake Waikaremoana
(lake views are from Panekire Bluff)*

*Korokoro
Falls*

*Forest scenes at
Waikaremoana*

Waikaremoana

certainly had! That night, two of the trampers drank a litre of wine each out of the four litres of wine they'd brought in.

They were soon joined by a group of twenty policemen who were also drinking. I was also offered a drink, which I declined. The hut was divided into four rooms which slept about 10–12 people, but I decided I really didn't want to sleep inside with all the drunken racket. It was a warm night, so I just took my mattress outside and went to sleep under the stars instead. I think alcohol consumption should be banned in DOC huts, or at least regulated to keep down the rowdiness, because there sure is a lot of it happening.

But even if such a policy were implemented, it would be difficult to enforce in the Waikaremoana area where DOC's presence is minimal at best. The reasons for this are tied in deep with the history of Te Urewera National Park, which was developed on land confiscated from Ngāi Tūhoe in the late 1860s.[44] This has been a contentious issue for the Tūhoe, and they have been wanting to obtain the entire area back ever since. I thought this was rightly deserved, but unfortunately many other people don't see it that way. The Tūhoe eventually received their land back in a historic deal settled by the Crown in 2012.[45]

The Tūhoe spokesperson Tāmati Kruger, who was one of the driving forces behind the historic deal, called for help; telling *New Zealand Wilderness Magazine* that his people didn't have all the resources needed to administer the park.[46] As a result of these issues and others, the Te Urewera Act was passed in 2014, an act which established Te Urewera as a legal person similar to a corporation, overseen by a board partly appointed by the Minister of Conservation and the Minister of Treaty of Waitangi Negotiations, and partly by Ngāi Tūhoe. In 2017, the board produced a draft management plan called *Te Kawa o Te Urewera*, which identifies Te Urewera as a living system. According to Kruger, "Te Urewera has its own identity that is legal, but also physical, environmental, cultural and spiritual."[47]

Kruger also notes that some of the Tūhoe don't want international tourists in the national park, which I believe would be a huge economic loss for both New Zealand and the area. However, concerns about tourism impact are also shared by others who work in other national parks, including some rangers I'd met on Ruapehu a few years ago, who thought that the whole thing was becoming too commercial.

The next day we continued our tramp, walking mostly downhill in the seven-and-a-half kilometre stretch from Panekire Hut to Waiopaoa Hut, which takes about three to four hours. This section of the tramp is filled with beech, podocarp and kāmahi trees, and it was just beautiful. From Waiopaoa Hut we carried on to Marauiti Hut for the second-longest stretch of walking through just over twelve kilometres of forest alongside the lake. This took us a little over five hours to complete, and along the way we passed some private baches owned by some renowned Hawkes Bay families, where we stopped and had lunch.

We had an uneventful stay at Marauiti Hut before the final stretch to Hopuruahine Landing, which, at 17 km, is easily the longest section of the Waikaremoana Track. Still, it was a lovely, moderate walk by the lakeside that only took us about half a day to complete. When we finally arrived at the landing, we decided to finish our tramp with a swim, which was very refreshing after the long day. After I got dressed, I met a local Māori woman who was looking after eight children and she told me that three of the Ngāi Tūhoe hapu or sub-tribes were fighting over the lakebed, which I thought was quite sad.

Our group was supposed to drive back together, but there was a disagreement, as some of the group wanted to carry onto Gisborne and go to one of the bars there. I ended up hitch-hiking back to Auckland instead because I didn't want to witness the big drinking session – what a way to finish my tramp on the Waikaremoana Track!

Postscript: the once-kidnapped Colin McCahon painting can be seen at the following permanent URL: http://www.mccahon.co.nz/cm001411

CHAPTER TWELVE

Mount Ruapehu

YOU CAN MAKE IT

Key Features in the Central Volcanic Area of the North Island.

Source: Public domain image from NASA Global Wind, accessed from URL https://commons.wikimedia.org/wiki/File:Tongariro_NP_satellite. jpg in February 2017. Text added for this book.

I 'VE had a long and interested association with Mount Ruapehu in the Tongariro National Park. The sprawling National Park area is hard to miss with its three volcanic peaks of Ruapehu, Tongariro and Ngauruhoe jutting out of the bare plains of the Desert Road in the Central North Island, just a few kilometres southwest of Lake Taupō. Because of its central location, I have visited Mount Ruapehu frequently, and as well as tramping in the area several times, I have also completed three mountaineering courses and worked as a volunteer DOC warden in one of the huts there for a week over Christmas.

I took my first snowcraft course on Mount Ruapehu in 2010 with a friend whom I shall call Bill. It was run by a lovely couple from the Auckland Tramping Club. There are a few members of the tramping club who, like them, tend to do a lot of volunteering behind the scenes and organise their own Christmas trips rather than going on the club's one.

We stayed in the club's hut on the mountain, Ruapehu Lodge, which is located on the Whakapapa side of the mountain near the ski fields and is an easy three-minute walk from the mountain access road, Bruce Road.

In the snowcraft course we learnt how to self-arrest – using an ice-axe to stop yourself falling down a cliff – and how to walk in crampons, spiked plates you attach to your boots for better grip on rocks and ice. These two skills are all you really need to start off with, though I still haven't camped out in the snow and had a chance to fully practice what I learnt.

There was a white-out on the mountain, so we could hardly see anything and it was bitterly cold. I felt it more than everyone else because my 'waterproof' pants leaked. Despite costing me $200 they weren't waterproof at all! I couldn't believe it. After the course finished I had to get another pair and found out you really have to get the right gear. It's important to get pants with the back reinforced so they don't leak.

After getting a taste for snowcraft on that course, I decided to do a Stage 2 course with the Hamilton Alpine Club, who were a great bunch. Most of them were rock-climbers learning how to be mountaineers. We stayed at their club hut and learnt belaying, which the rock-climbers took to with ease, but I wasn't confident because I've never managed to get the hang of knots.

After that, we had planned to hike to the top of Mt Ruapehu, but the organisers were going to cancel this because they thought it would be too windy. I put my foot down and told them I wanted to complete the course that I'd enrolled in, in which climbing to the peak was explicitly the final stage. I managed to convince most of the group, who really wanted to go, but the organisers weren't happy that I had made them do it.

We rode the ski field's chairlifts up as far as they go, and then hiked from there to the summit. From the last chairlift on Knoll Ridge, the climb is a five-hour return trip. The route is completely unformed with no markings, so it is up to each tramping party to find their own safe way to the top. We took the most commonly used route up Knoll Ridge and along the narrow foot track on Dome Ridge, stopping to get a photo at the shelter there. Because of the alpine risks, constant weather changes and icy conditions in winter, DOC recommends that the climb to the crater is only suitable for experienced trampers or those on guided walks. We made it to the crater, but it was hard, hot work, and the strong wind up there didn't make it any easier.

There was a Wellington teacher on that course who had bought alpine boots in Palmerston North after the store there let him take them home for a week and wear them in to see if they fitted. I thought that was a great idea because I've always had problems with my alpine boots fitting, so I asked a local company in Queenstown if I could try this but they wouldn't let me. It's a real issue because I've got bunions now and I've had three types of boots but never managed to find a pair that fitted perfectly.

The third course I did on Mt Ruapehu was on ice climbing, and was held by the New Zealand Alpine Club at the Tukino Alpine Sports Club Lodge on the remote eastern side of the mountain. I drove up there in my four-wheel drive and was instantly taken with the sheltered hut in its picturesque location overlooking the Tukino Ski Field. The New Zealand Alpine Club who I was to be ice climbing with were a lovely group of people. Their club sections are all different, with a lot of people simply organising their own groups to go climbing or tramping in the mountains. This felt like a foreign culture to me after being in so many tramping clubs where I was bullied, and it was wonderful to see a largely self-organised club where people had the freedom to do their own thing.

The woman who was training our group had a broken wrist, which made me worried as I didn't want to break any of my own bones! There was also a woman from Wellington in the group who had tried to get her photo in the *Wilderness Magazine* along with a couple of others and had suffered a major fall and had only just started ice climbing again. I also met a lovely 31-year-old Japanese man who later died on Mt Taranaki with his partner – such a sad loss, and one that really reinforces the dangers of alpine climbing.

All these injuries made me unsure about ice climbing, as I wanted to do it safely and without breaking anything. To make matters worse, I didn't have any decent ice-axes and had the wrong crampons for my boots, which made things difficult on the near-vertical slopes. It was a very mild winter and we were climbing an ice slope where I could see the water coming out and melting on the rocks, and that was the final straw. There was no way I was climbing on melting ice, it was too risky, and so I withdrew from the course the next day. I'd love to try it again, though, someday, but just doing basic climbing on a safer slope instead of trying to scale slippery slopes above rocks. I will go back and do a Stage 3 course.

The last time I was on Mt Ruapehu was in December 2014, when I did a stint as a volunteer DOC warden at the Whakapapaiti Hut for a week over Christmas. This hut is part of the Round-the-Mountain Track, a more remote alternative to the popular Northern Circuit. The Round-the-Mountain Track takes four to six days to complete and covers a loop of the mountain of just over 66 kilometres. I haven't done the full track yet, but I have done parts of it, including the 10.3-km walk between Whakapapaiti Hut and the next hut at Mangaturuturu, where there are beautiful views across to Mount Taranaki.

We stayed in the hut a night beforehand, and I met some women who were volunteering as DOC wardens in the other huts on the track. There was a young Korean woman from Auckland who was working there all summer and told the DOC officials that her mother had asked why she wasn't getting any food from them. There's no food in the huts for the wardens; they have to bring in all their own supplies. I knew that from my time in other DOC huts and brought plenty of food up with me. However, my hut was so sparse they didn't even have salt and pepper, which I thought was a little rude.

Still, the hut was beautiful and I loved being there over Christmas and waking up every morning to the beautiful view of Mount Ruapehu. The hut duties were fairly minimal: just keeping the place tidy, collecting the hut fees and staying in contact with the other wardens on the track with scheduled radio calls we had to make every morning.

I had some interesting people pass through my hut including two doctors and a policewoman. The doctors said they were running around the mountain to relieve a little of the stress in the build-up to Christmas and told me it was hard working over the holiday period because this period had the highest suicide and domestic violence rate out of the whole year. I think that shows the problems with Christmas and its excesses–that these health professionals were preparing for such a violent onslaught. The policewoman who passed through was running around the mountain for a similar reason

Beginning to get icicles in my hair

Hut buried by snow

and she told me, 'You have no idea of the cases we have to deal with on Christmas Day.' So, all these people were running around the mountain trying to relax before Christmas, and I thought, 'Good grief, this is supposed to be a happy time of year!'

Also staying in the hut was a fit-looking bus driver from Whangarei in his mid-sixties, who was planning to climb Mt Ruapehu. He stayed for four nights and, as we shared our food, he started telling me about how he used to work for DOC in their kiwi reserves. He would go around and trap rogue ferrets who had learnt how to kill adult kiwi birds and were threatening our already-rare native birds. However, he finished up at DOC ten years early because of personnel and management issues. I couldn't believe that someone like him with that much knowledge could be let go.

He knew all about the native bird life and talked enthusiastically about the blue duck breeding programme on Mount Ruapehu. I was lucky enough to see some in one of the nearby rivers. I also got to video them. Blue ducks – also known as whio – are one of the world's three species of torrent ducks, which means that they live in fast and unpolluted rivers in remote back-country and refuse to inhabit duckponds. The other two species of torrent duck live in New Guinea and South America respectively. I had no idea that there was such a thing as a duck that refuses to inhabit a pond, and of course this lifestyle has reduced the numbers of the whio relative to other sorts of ducks as New Zealand's landscape has become more domesticated.

DOC has made a huge effort to bring blue ducks back by breeding them in sheltered concrete areas with netting over the top to keep them protected. There are successful breeding programmes in the South Island as well, but I was blown away by the blue duck programme I saw at Mount Ruapehu. They breed around a hundred of these birds every year – a substantial number that must be one of the biggest breeding programmes in the country.

The bus driver was great company and I spent all Christmas Day talking to him. He told me about his family and his wife, who apparently didn't do a lot of tramping. He set off to climb Mount Ruapehu and invited me along, but I had a scheduled radio call that I would have missed if I'd gone. I might have made it, but I didn't feel like rushing to the summit and back so I just stayed at the hut.

Anyway, he made it to the top of Ruapehu despite not having any crampons, though when he got back he told me it had been fairly slippery.

He really should have had the right gear, as a pair of basic walking crampons is not that expensive.

The bus driver from Whangarei, at Mt Ruapehu

The Hamilton Alpine Club Hut at Mount Ruapehu on Bruce Road

NZ Alpine Club skills course

NZ Alpine Club skills course

169

CHAPTER THIRTEEN

Mt Tongariro and the Tongariro Crossing

A GEM

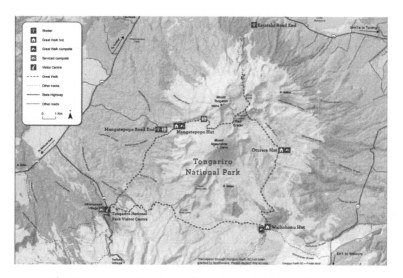

The Tongariro Northern Circuit and Alpine Crossing.

From Tongariro Northern Circuit (brochure), Wellington,
Department of Conservation, November 2016

W HILE Mount Ruapehu attracts skiers and ice-climbers to its slopes in the winter season, the northern, Mount Tongariro half of the Tongariro National Park provides opportunities for some serious tramping. Unlike the sheer peaks of Mount Ruapehu and Mount Ngauruhoe, Mount Tongariro has a series of spread-out slopes and craters and can be ascended as the one-day Alpine crossing, or as part of the longer three to four day Tongariro Northern Circuit, which is one of New Zealand's Great Walks.

171

(By the way, it is strongly, officially, recommended that anyone who is not a serious mountaineer should *not* attempt the Tongariro crossing, or circuit, in the more wintery months between early May and late October. The same goes for all New Zealand's Great Walks. They are only 'walks' in season.)

The wider Tongariro area, including Mounts Ngauruhoe and Ruapehu, was the first national park to be created in New Zealand when the powerful Ngāti Tūwharetoa tribe aligned their fortunes with the Crown and began to open up their lands for tourism in 1887. It is now one of a limited number of World Heritage Sites of joint natural and cultural significance.

Pākehā (Europeans) had been trying to venture into the area as early as 1839, but had been denied access because of the tapu on the summits of the sacred mountains, which prohibited outsiders. By the 1880s, the numbers of explorers trying to access the area was growing steadily, and the government had also asked for permission to survey the land for potential sheep-stocking. By 1886, they were using Ruapehu's summit for triangulation as well. That same year, Māori were allocated individual titles which lead to the sale of land that had been previously communally owned. Worried about the future of the Tongariro area, one of the paramount chiefs of Ngāti Tūwharetoa, Te Heuheu Tūkino, who is commonly and generally known as Te Heuheu, is recorded as having uttered the following moving words to his Pākehā son-in-law, Lawrence Grace, after a land court hearing:[48]

If our mountains of Tongariro are included in the blocks passed through the Court in the ordinary way, what will become of them? They will be cut up and perhaps sold, a piece going to one Pakeha and a piece to another. They will become of no account, for the tapu will be gone. Tongariro is my ancestor, my tupuna; it is my head; my mana centres around Tongariro.

Grace suggested that Te Heuheu make the peaks a "tapu place of the Crown" by gifting them to the government as a reserve that would be the property of all the people of New Zealand.[49] Te Heuheu accepted this advice, and by gifting his tribe's mountain lands to the Crown in 1887, prevented the desecration of Tongariro's iconic landmarks and set in motion the process that created the national park. The park opened seven years later, in 1894. The park has been stable since then, although I've been told that some of its peaks may not be available to trampers in the future with the ongoing negotiations between Māori and DOC.

I first tramped Tongariro in 2006 when I did the full Northern Circuit, and it was beautiful. From Whakapapa Village, we tramped eight and a half kilometres across the plains underneath the famous Mount Ngauruhoe, which some film buffs might recognise as Mount Doom from the *Lord of the Rings* trilogy. We stopped at Mangatepopo Hut at the entrance of the Tongariro Alpine Crossing, which we joined the following day, and hiked through to Oturere Hut – a five-hour walk of almost thirteen kilometres – passing the beautiful Emerald and Blue Lakes (the Blue Lake is also sacred or tapu to Māori, and needs to be treated similarly to a mountain peak). From Oturere it was a further three-hour walk to Waihohonu Hut, before the final stretch – a hike of just over fourteen kilometres through the Tama Saddle between Mt Ngauruhoe and Mt Ruapehu – to return to our starting point at Whakapapa Village.

After my first day on the Tongariro Northern Circuit, I had already fallen in love with the area and promised myself I'd come back to explore it further. After my snowcraft course on the nearby Mount Ruapehu in 2010 with the Auckland Tramping Club, I thought I'd make the most of my time in the national park and headed over to tramp the start of the one-day Tongariro Alpine Crossing. I joined two other guys, Terry and Brian, from the club who had planned to climb to Ketatahi Hut on Mt Tongariro. They were very nice guys who I got on well with, so it was a good little tramping party.

We tramped up over the central crater of Tongariro, where the snow was quite deep. I soon learnt that hiking with crampons on becomes easier if you follow in the footsteps of the person in front of you. The walk had steep drops, and we had to self-arrest with our ice-axes several times to stop ourselves falling down them, so I was thankful we'd learnt how to do it properly on the snowcraft course. Brian's crampon came off in the snow, which was pretty dangerous, so we left him to adjust it and carried on to the hut where he later caught us up. We were all tired and no one could work out how to use the heater, so the hut was freezing and there was even snow and ice inside. The night was so cold that the next morning I took off early at 6.30 am and tramped three hours over the summit to the hot Soda Springs. I knew I was violating Māori protocol as the Soda Springs are considered tapu and they've tried to get rid of the track to it, but I really needed to warm up. I tramped back to Ketatahi Hut where the others had finally managed to get the heater going, so we all managed to make it out without getting hypothermia!

Despite the cold, the tramp to Ketatahi Hut was well worth it, with magnificent views of Lake Rotoaira, Mount Pihanga and even the distant Lake Taupō. The hut is now a museum and shelter, as the greater part of it was destroyed in 2012 when the mountain erupted. I was there at the time, as I was planning to climb Mount Tongariro when the Te Maari crater blew.

All the volcanic mountains in the Tongariro National Park are still active. So, in addition to the usual hazards you have when tramping in mountainous areas, there's also the added risk of volcanic activity. As such, DOC recommends that all trampers intending to trek the crossing should

*On the snowy Tongariro Alpine Crossing in 2011
with the Auckland Tramping Club*

Red Crater

The top of Mount Ngauruhoe

Yaquoob, 2016

*Emerald Lakes
and wilderness
signpost*

The Oturere Valley and a view of Lake Rotoaira

check in on the current volcanic alert level of the mountains at one of their offices, or online, before setting out.

In 2011, I tramped to the Ketatahi Hut for a second time before it was destroyed, again with the Auckland Tramping Club. We tramped the whole Tongariro Crossing, staying in Mangatepopo Hut for the first night and Ketatahi Hut the second night. It was a four to five-hour tramp between the huts, covering around seventeen kilometres on the snowbound Tongariro Track.

However, we didn't start our walk until late because one 75-year-old grandfather was sick and we had to wait for an hour. In between bouts of throwing up, he told us his wife was skiing on Mt Ruapehu, which wasn't far away. I suggested his wife could come and pick him up as he wasn't well. I wasn't forgiven for that comment, although I thought it was fair as I hadn't come all that way to not go tramping. At the time, he certainly didn't seem up for it, and there were ten of us waiting.

With that group was another older lady, a grandmother of nearly eighty who was wearing makeup on the mountain and made her son, in his fifties, carry her pack. I heard her tell her son that if he didn't help her up the mountain she would leave him out of the will! She was fully determined to complete the crossing, and had even done a Stage One snowcraft course in preparation, which I thought was incredible at her age. Later, I asked her what encouraged her to go tramping, and she said, 'I'm sick of sitting at home. My husband died two years ago, and I'm bored. I just want to accomplish some things before I die!' With makeup and grey hair, she looked like quite the lady, but she seemed well at home in the mountains and even managed to self-arrest with her ice axe when she slipped on the Tongariro slopes during our tramp.

The third time I tramped through Tongariro was with the Auckland Meetup group in 2012. The tramping party was about eighteen in total, many of whom had never been on an overnight tramp before. We didn't go to Ketatahi Hut, but ended up walking most of the Northern Circuit, staying in the Mangatepopo, Oturere and Waihohonu Huts before finishing up at the Whakapapa Visitor Centre.

On the tramp was one couple, a Chinese woman and a South African man, who were having relationship difficulties. Although he absolutely loved her, she wasn't willing to have children with him. I caught a lift down to Tongariro with them and tried to maintain the peace between them, but things got even worse when we started tramping. Apparently, she'd never hiked with a pack before because the one time they'd been tramping before was in Namibia and they had just hired servants to carry their packs. She kept screaming that it hurt and she hated it, which I couldn't handle so I just walked ahead.

There were a few others who left early on that tramp as well, pulling out after the first day and heading back. They hadn't drunk enough water and got low on energy, so it was for the best. However, one who didn't pull out but surprised me by making the whole tramp, was Frank, who was a bit of a computer nerd with really thick, goggly glasses. The first time I had met him was at the Meetup group, and he had offered me a disgustingly chewy chocolate ball which he'd made. I told him I didn't eat chocolate but I'd try one under pressure, and after doing so told him they were horrible just to see his reaction!

Anyway, as it turned out, Frank had quite a sad past. He had five children back in the USA and had come out to New Zealand in 2009 to try and set up a new life. At the start, he'd owned several houses in the States, but a rogue property manager had stolen the rent money and, because he was overseas in New Zealand, he just lost everything.

He had come on the tramp with two packs and a very large tent which he asked if I wanted to sleep in even though I had brought my own tent. He'd brought enough food in for everyone as well, despite us all having our own food, and asked us to carry half of it up for him. In amongst the food, I saw he'd brought about seven or eight bags of chips, which was unbelievable as junk food really isn't a good idea while hiking. I was beginning to wonder if he'd ever been tramping before! Still, all of us from Auckland really liked Frank – he was such a character and really made the walk fun.

Once we reached the far side of the Northern Circuit near Tama Saddle, we did a short side trip of around twenty minutes to the historic Waihohonu Hut. When the first Waihohonu Hut was erected in 1904 it was the first hut built in the area, and was used until 1968 when it was replaced by the current Waihohonu Hut. We saw graffiti and old skis there from the early 1900s. The whole place is treated with respect, and really, it's just like a museum of early New Zealand tramping that would be lost to New Zealand tourism if it had to be upgraded further. Although a lot of tourists do complete the Northern Circuit, which I did in 2006 and again on this tramp, a lot of them don't explore much further into the national park, which keeps areas like Waihohonu well-preserved. I hope it stays this way, because I really love the area. In summer, the sun reflects off the Emerald Lakes and Blue Lakes, and the flatlands near the azure Tama Lakes remind me of a desert. It really is one of the most stunning places in the world.

Most recently, in June 2016 – that is to say, during the wintery time of year not recommended for anyone who is not a skilled mountaineer – I did the Tongariro Alpine Crossing with a friend of mine named Yaquoob from Kashmir, and I have some wonderful photos of the Emerald and Blue Lakes as a result.

There were 65-knot winds when we set out, but I love the grasses and the smell on Tongariro when you first start out and don't mind the weather. When it's wet, the grasses change colour. We did the crossing coming from the other side in the strong winds. When we went past the Red Crater my friend was very scared even though DOC have put up ropes there to hold onto. My friend was unsteady on his feet and duly petrified, as in Kashmir they use mules to carry the packs.

CHAPTER FOURTEEN
Lakes Rotoaira and Rotopounamu

Aerial image showing locations of Lake Rotoaira and the smaller Lake Rotopounamu near the red highway shield marked '47'.

Source: Google Earth, imagery ©2017 DigitalGlobe, Waikato District Council, Horizons Regional Consortium, Map Data ©2017 Google.

ALSO well worth a visit are Lakes Rotoaira and Rotopounamu, two beautiful lakes which lie halfway between the volcanoes of Tongariro National Park and Lake Taupō. Though Lake Rotoaira, which officially stands at 564 metres above sea level, has been modified for hydroelectric purposes and stocked with introduced trout, both lakes are nonetheless surrounded by native bush. A walking track off State Highway 47 goes all the way around the smaller of the two lakes, Rotopounamu; which stands at an altitude of 716 metres. Both lakes are closely overlooked by the bald-topped Mount Pihanga, visible at centre-right in the aerial photograph above, at 1,326 metres.

On the north side of Lake Rotoaira, and all the way around Lake Rotopounamu, there is continuous native bush in an outlying exclave of Tongariro National Park containing Rotopounamu and Pihanga.

On the south side of Lake Rotoaira, south of State Highway 46, there is quite a different ecosystem just back from the lake, the Rotoaira Forest, which is a commercial plantation of pine. If you look closely at the aerial photograph on the previous page, you can see that the Rotoaira Forest has a grid of logging roads in it. If the Rotoaira forest were to be harvested and native forest or bush allowed to regrow, the Tongariro National Park could extend continuously across this area.

*Lakes Rotoaira and
Rotopounamu area*

Tree near Lake Rotoaira, and Lake Taupo as seen from the same area

CHAPTER FIFTEEN

Rotorua, Taupō, and the Thermal Region

Rotorua, Taupō and the Thermal Region. Note the 'line of fire' from White Island to Taupō and beyond to the large volcanoes of the central North Island.

Map data ©2017 Google; name of White Island added for this book.

No account of New Zealand would be complete without a description of the Rotorua thermal region and Lake Taupō. This is a part of New Zealand that is highly accessible to tourists and holidaymakers and very well covered in other travel memoirs and guidebooks, whereas in this book, I am really writing about places that are more adventurous or off the beaten track. Nevertheless, Rotorua was one of New Zealand's original tourist destinations both for cultural and spa-town reasons, and is well worth visiting for a more traditional tourism experience. The same is true of Taupō, an inland great lake popular with yachties and trout-fishers.

A Māori Jesus, St. Faith's, Ohinemutu, Rotorua.

Rotorua and Taupō both lie on a 'line of fire' that runs from White Island through to Tongariro National Park. The whole Rotorua region is a caldera similar to Yellowstone National Park in the USA, and Taupō is of similarly explosive origin, though there are fewer boiling springs in the immediate vicinity as compared to Rotorua.

Marble Terrace (Sinter Terrace) in Waimangu Volcanic Valley.

Public Domain Image by 'Pseudopanax', URL https://commons.
wikimedia.org/wiki/File:Marble_Terrace_(sinter_terrace)_in_
Waimangu_Volcanic_Valley.jpg

Portal, Rotorua Museum of Art and History / Te Whare Taonga o Te Arawa

Yachts on Lake Taupō, with volcanoes of Tongariro National Park in the background

CHAPTER SIXTEEN
Mt Taranaki
ONE OF OUR DEADLIEST MOUNTAINS

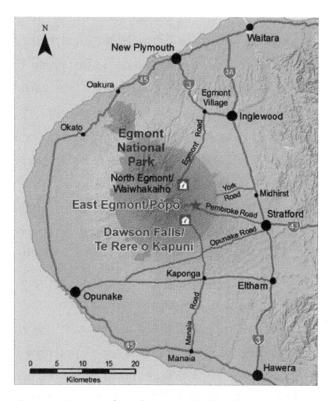

Egmont National Park, containing Mount Taranaki.

From Dawson Falls and East Egmont Walks (brochure),
Wellington, Department of Conservation, November 2015.

T HE last of the North Island's large volcanoes is the lone Mount
Taranaki, which is about a three-hour drive towards the west from
Tongariro National Park. I've climbed Mount Taranaki twice, from both the

Summit Track (near New Plymouth) and the Dawson Falls/East Egmont Track, which is near the small town of Stratford.

The mountain must cause some confusion for overseas visitors as it commonly goes by two names: the traditional Māori name is Taranaki, while Captain Cook in his early explorations of New Zealand renamed it Egmont after a British lord. The mountain and its slopes form a national park which is officially known as Egmont National Park, though the mountain is generally now known as Taranaki by Māori and Pākehā alike.

As with other prominent peaks, Mount Taranaki was considered sacred in Māori tradition. According to the relevant Department of Conservation literature, current as of early 2017, "Visitors are asked to show respect by not standing directly on the summit peak, not camping or cooking on or around the summit, and removing all rubbish."

When the New Zealand government began purchasing land for settlers in the mid-nineteenth century, Taranaki Māori refused to let their communally-owned land go up for sale.[50] The government tried to force land sales and escalated the situation by making war in 1860, which they used as an excuse to confiscate the land of Māori who were deemed 'rebellious'.

After the wars, it was realised that Mount Taranaki was an important area, both for its significance to Māori and for its potential for tourism, and so the Egmont National Park was established in 1900. It was only the second national park to be created in New Zealand after Tongariro, and government initiatives to cut tracks and build huts helped to encourage outdoor recreation in the area.[51]

It was quite a hot day and the walk certainly didn't become easier once we passed Tahurangi Lodge and got onto the steep scree (loose gravel) slopes. While I hadn't climbed many mountains at that time, and Rose hadn't done any tramping for fifteen years, I think Daniel really had the hardest time with it. He sat down halfway up and said there weren't very many high mountains like this in Fiji, where he was from. Indeed, the highest mountain in Fiji, Mount Tomanivi, is only a bit over half as high as Taranaki and forested all the way to the top. Climbing in scree above the low New Zealand treeline is really quite difficult, because for every step up, you slide back at least half of it in the loose ground, so it's just a constant up-and-down battle to make even a few metres.

We finally made it up onto the Lizard, a more stable rocky ridge, and then from there it was only another few hundred metres of climbing to the summit. We stopped for a short break after the exhausting scree slopes, then carried on to the summit, and I thought Daniel had done very well to make it. I enjoyed the tramp, and the view from the top of Mt Taranaki was beautiful – over the clouds we could even see the distant Mt Ruapehu.

The next time I was on Mt Taranaki was in 2014 with Bill to climb to Fanthams Peak from the Dawson Falls/East Egmont side. We arrived in Stratford at around nine o'clock at night, and Bill wanted to stay in a hotel in New Plymouth, which I thought was a terrible idea. I looked in the New Zealand Alpine Club journals for information about the east side of Mt Taranaki and found there was a hut owned by the Mt Egmont Alpine Club that was only an hour away from the Dawson Falls carpark. This Alpine Club is separate from the more national New Zealand Alpine Club, and was founded in 1928 by Rod Syme to promote outdoor activities on Mt Taranaki. They did this by building huts and arranging club trips to the area.

We called up the club and managed to book the hut. We set off hiking at ten o'clock and made it to the hut at eleven. We were let into the beautiful, largely unused Kapuni Lodge by the chairperson of the club – a lovely woman whose name was Maria (I think). I should have kept her contacts because the Mt Egmont Alpine Club seemed like the sort of people I could

The almost perfect cone of Mount Taranaki

A view of the Tongariro National Park volcanoes in the distance from Mount Taranaki

Mount Taranaki from the air, Fanthams Peak in the foreground

go out tramping with in the future. As she showed us around the hut, she told us to take care on the mountain and we fell to talking about the couple who had recently died on the mountain, in October 2013. That was the Japanese man I had met at Tukino Lodge on Mt Ruapehu when I went on

The edge of the Egmont National Park is clearly visible as an arc in this view from Mount Taranaki

Intersection of tracks to Lake Dive and Dawson Falls

the ice-climbing course. He and his girlfriend, a New Zealander, had been on a tramp which had been organised by another club. I had been very tempted to go on the same tramp, but for some strange reason I didn't.

The grassy slopes heading up towards the summit

Fanthams Peak with Syme Hut visible on the near-side crater sim

Towards the
Summit

At the summit. Mount Ruapehu can be just glimpsed in the centre distance of the central photograph.

The couple had left at two o'clock in the afternoon and became separated from the group up on the Lizard in a terrible storm – very common on Mount Taranaki due to its exposed location, jutting westward into the Tasman Sea – and tried to build a snow cave to shelter from the weather.[52] They had been in contact with the police and their families, but rescue services had been unable to find them because of the weather, and they spent two days stranded out on the mountain. The rescue services had gone into action within an hour of the couple going missing because of Taranaki's reputation for bad weather. The man had died, tragically sheltering his girlfriend in a snow-cave that was only waist-deep and provided little shelter from the storm. Though still talking when she was found, the girlfriend deteriorated and also died on the mountain a few hours later.

I knew friends of friends who went to his funeral, and the unfortunate leader from the club was blamed for not looking after the tramping party. However, people do take a certain amount of personal responsibility when they're mountain climbing and I certainly wouldn't blame the leader. The Japanese man was a very good mountaineer, but why he ignored the weather forecast and continued to try and head towards the summit is beyond me. You must respect the mountain and *always* be aware of the conditions when tramping or mountain climbing, no matter how high or low the summit is.

More than eighty climbers have died on the slopes of Mount Taranaki since the first recorded instance of such a fatality in 1891;[53] to which must be added the victims of several military and light aircraft collisions with the prominent peak. A common denominator to many of these fatalities has been the weather, particularly changeable even by the standards of the rest of New Zealand and its mountains. A fine sunny day with good visibility on the ground and in the air can turn into a 'whiteout' a few minutes later.

Moreover, because of its steep contours, you can't build adequately deep snow caves for shelter on most parts of Mount Taranaki (that was the problem for the two climbers I just mentioned). And if you slip on Mount Taranaki, or get lost in mist, there is also a danger of going over one of its many lava bluffs.

The facts of steepness and prominence above the surrounding landscape, bluffs, a low tree-line and changeable weather can easily turn Mount Taranaki into a death-trap for those on the ground and in the air. And the fact that the mountain is highly accessible and not considered technically difficult to ascend only baits the trap further.

Having said all that, between six and eight thousand people were climbing Mount Taranaki each year a decade ago, and one media story claims that fifteen thousand climb the mountain each year now.[54,55] So, while Taranaki has been described as a 'Cone of Catastrophes',[56] in part because of its reputation as a magnet for disoriented pilots, it's actually rather surprising that more climbers haven't also come to grief on the mountain.

We stayed the night in Kapuni Lodge and left at eight o'clock the next morning to climb to the summit. Despite having climbed Taranaki before and Mt Ruapehu a few years ago, Bill was unfit and was breathless most of the way up – no wonder he had wanted to stay at a motel! I left him behind and followed the trail a few hours up to Syme Hut on Fanthams Peak. This smaller, subsidiary cone of Mt Taranaki wasn't explored until 1887, when it was named after the first woman to stand on its summit, nineteen-year-old Fanny Fantham.[57] The Syme Hut which perches on its slopes was first built by the Mt Egmont Alpine Club in 1930 before being replaced in 1980 by the current DOC-managed hut.

It was hard going up to Fanthams Peak and I had to use my ice axe on the rocks; a technique known as dry-tooling. I lost my breath getting up, but made it to the top and looked down and saw that the clouds were coming in fast towards the mountain. There were four Koreans up the top who had a GPS, and they asked me if I wanted to go down with them so we could use the GPS to get safely through the cloud, but I decided to head down by myself instead. The view was beautiful up there, especially looking towards the Taranaki Summit, but I didn't stay long as I was worried I'd be clouded in.

I made it back to Bill, who wanted to know how I'd been able to climb up there and he couldn't. Well, if you're unfit, mountain climbing is obviously going to be difficult! I try and maintain my fitness by walking a total of one day a week, but at the moment I'm only walking half a day a week. Still, before attempting anything like Mount Taranaki, I'd do at least one multi-day hike.

(By the way, Mount Taranaki and Egmont National Park are not the only attractions in the Taranaki region. There are wild surf beaches out west; and on the sunny, northern side of the Taranaki peninsula there is the port city of New Plymouth, which won three major awards in 2008 from the United Nations-sponsored organisation LiveCom including a prize for being the most liveable city with a population between 25,000 and 75,000.[58] Along with its coastal walkaway, a major factor in the LiveCom awards, New Plymouth can also be proud of Pukekura Park, a mixture of gardens and natural wilderness preserved in the heart of the city since 1876 and quite a special place. The adjacent Bowl of Brooklands, a sort of natural amphitheatre, regularly plays host to international outdoor performances including the WOMAD festival, short for World of Music, Arts and Dance.)

CHAPTER SEVENTEEN

The Rugged Interior

WHANGANUI, THE KAIMANAWAS, RUAHINES AND
TARARUAS

J UST lately, I came across an diary of travels in old-time New Zealand
called *In the Land of the Tui*. Published in London in the 1890s, the
diary was kept by a woman named Eliza Wilson who confessed, on the first
page, that "From early childhood in theory I have been a Bohemian; to go
everywhere has been my one passionate longing. . . "[59] So I am not the first
Maverick Traveller even in my own sense of the phrase, it would seem!

At one point, the redoubtable Mrs. Wilson mentions a curious fact that is
still an aspect of New Zealand life today. After running into some Auckland
polo players at Christchurch's Riccarton Racecourse, she wrote that:

We very rarely meet any residents of Auckland so far south, and it has been
pleasant to hear something of that portion of these islands which seems
as remote as though it were in another sphere. It is odd that a town, so
recently the seat of Government [Auckland was the capital of New Zealand
from 1842 until 1865], should now have become strange to the rest of the
Colony; but so it is; Wellington, Christchurch and Dunedin are always *en
rapport*, but Auckland appears distant and separate.

There is a very good reason why this was so, and why it remains so. The
reason lies in the extraordinary ruggedness of a belt of terrain that stretches
all the way from Taranaki, at the westward extension of the North Island,
to East Cape at its eastern-most end. This belt of rugged terrain is caused by

203

the collision of tectonic plates, the Australian and the Pacific, and it isolates Auckland from the rest of the country almost as effectively as a larger or more obvious mountain range would.

Both of the North Island's two largest rivers originate in this belt, which includes Lake Waikaremoana, Lake Taupō and the large volcanoes of the central North Island. The Waikato River flows northward from Lake Taupō to reach the sea south of Auckland. The other of these two big rivers, the Whanganui, originates near Lake Rotoaira and flows northward, then westward, and finally southward to the sea at Whanganui, a distance of 290 kilometres.

For most of its northward course the Waikato flows through fairly accessible terrain. The Whanganui, on the other hand, flows through a sort of 'land that time forgot', through which the appropriately named Forgotten World Highway, a mostly gravel road, also runs for 148 km between Taumurunui and Stratford. Both of those are sizeable towns, but the largest town between them is Whangamomona, a tiny, Wild West-like outpost where the locals might easily be outnumbered by tourists on a good day. Though mainly used by cycle tourists (mountain bikes are best) the Forgotten World Highway can be driven by car; but it pays to fill up first and I wouldn't take a really flash car down that road.

The Whanganui River is popular with canoeists who paddle or float down its innumerable bends in an otherwise utterly inaccessible terrain.

As with Lake Waikaremoana, much of the North Island interior is steeped in Māoritanga, and the Wanganui River is no exception.

The river 'stars' in the 1981 film *Pictures*, a highly atmospheric dramatization of the lives of the Burton Brothers, pioneering photographers of nature, colonial architecture and the Māori for whom no part of the New Zealand landscape was too wet or steep to lug an old-fashioned

The Rugged Interior of the North Island. Images above and below are not to the same scale; the locality of Putere is common to both and highlighted in an orange rectangle in both cases.

Imagery ©2017 Landsat/Copernicus, Data SIO, NOAA, US Navy, NGA, GEBCO. Data LDEO-Columbia, NSF, NOAA. Map data ©2017 Google.

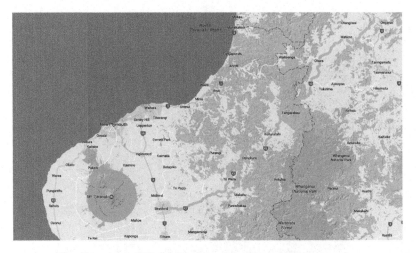

The Forgotten World Highway. Map data ©2017 Google.

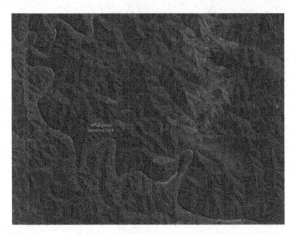

A Section of the Whanganui River.
Imagery ©2017 CNES / Astrium, DigitalGlobe, Map data ©2017 Google.

camera into. The Whanganui and its people were also the subject of a well-made government documentary from the 1950s called *The Legend of the Whanganui River*. James K. Baxter, who is probably New Zealand's greatest

*Wellington, the Tararua Range
and Environs.*

Imagery ©2017 Landsat/Copernicus, Data SIO,
NOAA, US Navy, NGA, GEBCO. Data LDEO-
Columbia, NSF, NOAA, Terrametrica. Map data
©2017 Google.

poet, ended up in a small village on the Whanganui in his later years; a site
of pilgrimage to some people still.

A notoriously unsuccessful attempt to settle European farmers in this area
is commemorated by the 'Bridge to Nowhere', a bridge at the end of a road
that leads to – well – to what some people would consider to be nowhere.

The whole of this interior terrain, right through to the East Coast, is a
site for adventures, including rafting and canoeing on wild rivers such as
the Motu, which flows down to the Bay of Plenty. These rivers are shorter
than the Whanganui – but they are also steeper.

Wild horses inhabit some of the more steppe-like parts of this terrain,
in the vicinity of the Kaimanawa Range just east of the large volcanoes of

the Tongariro National Park. From the Kaimanawa Range low mountains also run southward to form the Ruahine Range and then, south of the Manawatu Gorge where a river rises to the east of the range and flows west through a great crack in the earth, the Tararua Range and its foothills around Wellington such as the Akatarawa and the Rimutaka Ranges.

There is much more that I could say about the North Island. But it is now time to turn the page and to move on to the second half of the book: The South Island.

PART II
THE SOUTH ISLAND

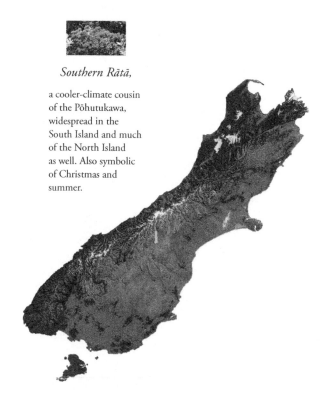

Southern Rātā,

a cooler-climate cousin
of the Pōhutukawa,
widespread in the
South Island and much
of the North Island
as well. Also symbolic
of Christmas and
summer.

The South Island of New Zealand

Source: detail from the NASA Earth Observatory image 2010/099

CHAPTER EIGHTEEN

Queen Charlotte Track

A COASTAL STROLL WITH THE BIRDS

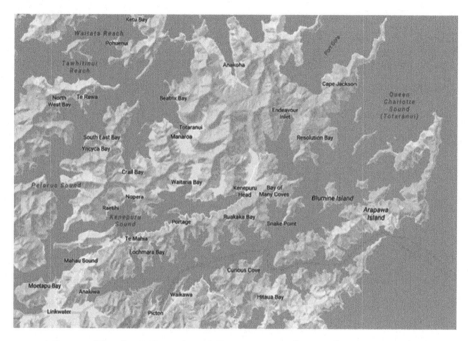

Queen Charlotte Sound and Environs, at the north-eastern end of the South Island. Source: Google Maps. Map data ©2017 Google

I TRAMPED the Queen Charlotte Track during summer. This track follows the length of the Queen Charlotte Sound, officially Queen Charlotte Sound / Tōtaranui, at the top of the South Island. There's no road to the beginning of the track at Meretoto / Ship Cove, so all trampers must be dropped off here by boat from Picton and can choose to hike with their gear or have it transported by one of the many water taxi companies in the area. Anyway, what I really enjoyed about the track was the fact that they sold wooden walking sticks along it for trampers to use (which I thought was a fantastic idea), and that there were several private places where you could stay. From the track, you are also able to see both the east and west coasts' sunrises and sunsets.

The Queen Charlotte Sound is one of the main inlets in the Marlborough Sounds, a vast network of sea-drowned valleys that forms the entranceway to the South Island. The area was first settled by Māori around 800 years ago, and they built villages and made canoe voyages through the sound. Queen Charlotte Sound was sighted by the explorer Abel Tasman and then by Captain Cook in their voyages to New Zealand.

Captain Cook named the sound after the wife of King George III, Queen Charlotte of Mecklenburg-Strelitz. Cook made Queen Charlotte Sound a base of operations in his three voyages to New Zealand, anchoring by preference in the bay he called Ship Cove, already known to Māori as a good long-term anchorage under the name of Meretoto.

In the 1800s the Marlborough area was settled by Europeans who mostly confined themselves to Picton, although a small mining town sprang up in Endeavour Inlet during the 1880s. The three to five-day hike along the coast is a comfortable walk, and can be a great alternative to the overcrowded Abel Tasman Track.

I was dropped off by the ferry at Meretoto, and after stopping to admire the memorial to Captain Cook, I began the track by climbing through fifteen kilometres of forested ridges and crossing Endeavour Inlet to reach Kenepuru Saddle Campsite, a walk of around nine hours. I stayed at the Kenepuru Saddle where the dawn chorus of birds was the best I've heard in the country.

The bird life on the track was loud and natural. I saw so many different kinds, and it's not very often that I've experienced a dawn chorus such as that. In Auckland, around where I live, the tūī imitate burglar alarms and garage doors – not quite the same!

Amongst the birds were some feisty weka, a brown, flightless bird native to New Zealand, and I managed to get some fantastic photos of them. They were running into the campsites and stealing food… which wasn't funny. There was a family with about four kids camping there and one weka just went into their tent and stole their bags of muesli, taking their entire breakfast for a week.

Parts of the track were open grass plains and I found them quite hard to handle in the hot summer weather. It was hard going in my thick, leather tramping boots and merino socks and I do remember getting blisters here. From the campsite near Kenepuru Saddle, I hiked up to Eatwell's Lookout where the signpost to the major cities of the world is secondary to the stunning views of the Sounds. After this steep climb, I followed the ridges along for another twenty kilometres or so to Torea Saddle with views of Queen Charlotte Sound and Kenepuru Sound. The next day I followed the track for seven and a half kilometres through to the picturesque Lochmara Bay, which took around four hours, and from there it was another four hours before I came out at Anakiwa. I was amazed by this small, coastal village hiding at the edge of the Queen Charlotte Sound – it was beautiful. I stayed with a friend who owned property there, and then hitchhiked down to the nearby town of Havelock, which is about eighteen kilometres away.

I caught a lift with a truck driver and we got stuck behind some cyclists who were taking up the road. The truck driver cursed all cyclists and said that if they didn't get off their bikes, he was going to bowl them over. He had a huge logging truck and the roads were very narrow. That was the first time in my life I saw cyclists get off their bikes and give way to a truck. I guess they could tell he wasn't worth tangling with, but I thought the mentality of the truck driver left something to be desired.

Weka

Cook Memorial

Kenepuru Sound

Eatwell's Lookout

Lochmara Bay

CHAPTER NINETEEN
Abel Tasman Coast Track
VARIED TERRAIN AND KAYAKING

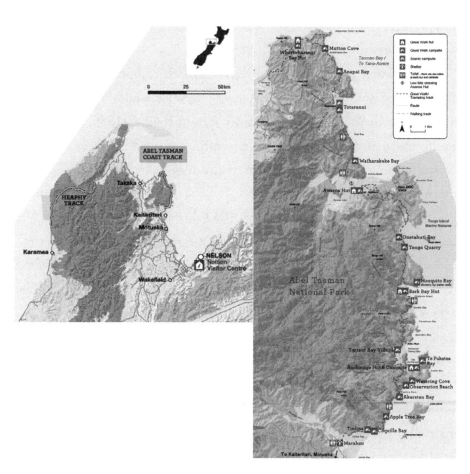

The Abel Tasman Coast Track.

From Abel Tasman Coast Track (brochure), Wellington,
Department of Conservation, September 2016

I FIRST tramped the Abel Tasman Coast Track in 1998, and revisited it in 2000, with brief visits since, most recently in 2017. In 1998, I had been very stressed out so it was nice to relax while hiking through this amazing stretch of New Zealand coastline. Located in the Abel Tasman National Park at the northern end of the South Island, the sixty-kilometre track takes around three to five days to hike, but can be shortened by taking a kayak or water taxi between beaches.

The national park is named after the Dutch explorer Abel Janszoon Tasman, who was the first European to visit New Zealand when he anchored his two ships in Wainui Bay, near Golden Bay, in 1642. In 1855, a settlement was founded and its great logging enterprises ravaged the forests and the coastal areas until concerned conservationists helped the land become protected by the Crown.

The national park was gazetted in 1942 during the low point of WWII largely due to the efforts of a local conservationist and bird-lover, Pérrine Moncrieff née Millais (1893-1979), an English-born grand-daughter of the famous English painter of that name John Everett Millais and his wife Effie, who was previously the wife of the still more famous art critic John Ruskin, by way of their son Everett Millais.

One of their other sons, the naturalist John Guille Millais, encouraged his niece Pérrine to study science (unusual for a girl in those days, perhaps) and she eventually became an ornithologist, an expert on birdlife. Pérrine married a British military officer named Malcolm Matthew Moncrieff in 1914, and after the war, which her husband survived, the couple had a holiday in New Zealand and decided to stay as they were both keen naturalists and appreciated the beauty and unique qualities of the New Zealand outdoors, including its bird-based ecology.

It was J. E. and Effie's grand-daughter Pérrine's suggestion to celebrate the 300th anniversary of Tasman's landing by creating the park named after him.[60]

By the way, the posh background of the Moncrieffs is not that unusual among early New Zealand colonists or even some who came later. Frontier stereotypes notwithstanding, not every New Zealand colonist was a rough character fond of pulling a cork in some honky-tonk saloon; nor for that matter someone poor but respectable driven out of the old country by grinding hardship and not being allowed to catch the fish in the river that belonged to the local lord.

People who were *really* poor generally couldn't afford to come all the way out to New Zealand in the first place; while those whose passage was furnished for free by the British government mostly went to Australia, as everyone knows.

The fact is that many people who were quite refined came out to New Zealand in the early days. Sometimes they did so in search of a political utopia like the Wakefields; or because they were keen naturalists like the Moncrieffs; or because they had been caught up in some sort of Victorian scandal themselves; or because, like Samuel Butler, the author while in New Zealand of *Erewhon* and the Christchurch-published essays 'Darwin among the Machines' and 'Lucubratio Ebria', because they had a modest fortune in the bank and the intention of rapidly multiplying it.

That last object was difficult back home, but easier on an under-developed frontier where you could invest the money in lambs and watch them turn into sheep while grazing on land that didn't seem to belong to anyone in particular –there were a lot of places like that in the South Island at one time – while dashing off the next novel or essay or watercolour painting, or making some new discovery in a landscape still unfamiliar to science.

Marahau

Other beach scenes

As with the Moncrieffs, it seems that a greater proportion of these educated sorts of settlers ended up in the Nelson region than elsewhere. Nelson is a sort of utopia for freethinkers, which has long prided itself, just quietly, on that claim. Indeed, right now, there are also twelve rural communes in the Nelson and Takaka districts at present, the earliest of which, the Riverside Community, was founded as far back as 1941.

Like most Great Walks, the Abel Tasman Coast Track can be hiked from either end, either starting from Marahau, which is just under seventy kilometres from Nelson, or Wainui Bay, which is just over twenty kilometres from Takaka. The gentle coastal walk is largely flat and has many campsites, making it a family-friendly trek that can be walked by trampers of all levels, unlike some of the more mountainous Great Walks. Because of this, it is a particularly popular walk, especially over the summer months.

When I did it in October, 1998, I couldn't get over the number of possums on the track. It was a beautiful coastal walk but it just seemed to be infested with possums. Every time you camped out, even if it was on the beach, there would be around 40 possums sitting in the trees at night watching you when you got up to go to the toilet. People would get up and try to throw stones at them to scare them away, but they kept hanging around. I didn't know whether to hang my food in the trees or keep it in my tent, but after seeing that many of the pests in the bush, I decided my tent would be safer.

I tramped on to Tōtaranui, which is fifteen and a half kilometres from Wainui Bay, and decided to sleep out on the beach. Even there the possums tried to get into my tent and would stalk around and around it at night. Thankfully, none got inside because apparently when they get caught in tents they can become quite vicious and it's very hard to get them out.

Whariwharangi Beach and Whariwharangi Hut. Also, a resurgent population of Pūkeko and Weka at Tōtarani in 2017. No dogs are allowed!

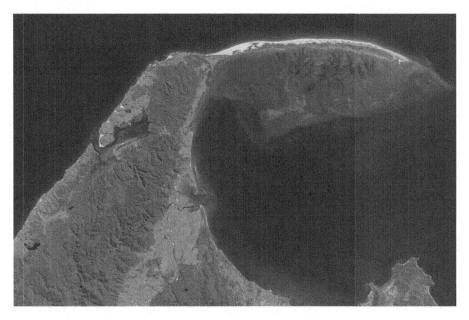

Farewell Spit and Environs. (Nasa Earth Observatory image 2001044, captured by the ASTER satellite on 13 February 2001)

There was also evidence of other pests in the area, especially stoats – I couldn't believe there was so much stoat poo on the track! Trying to avoid the dung, I tramped on for about three hours to Whariwharangi Bay where I saw the old Whariwharangi Hut. This hut was built around 1896 and used to be an old homestead. What a beautiful place. I'd love to go back in the winter and do the track if it was lightly covered with snow – it'd look great if it was snowing I think. Unfortunately snow only very rarely falls in the region. Golden Bay and Nelson form a Riviera coast which faces toward the sun and is protected from the cold south winds that bring snow to New Zealand by the mountainous spine of the South Island. It is sheltered from westerlies, too. The region is in consequence warmer and sunnier than many places in the North Island.

221

After Whariwharangi, I continued by kayak, which gave me a 3-D perspective of the coast. The kayaks on the beach at Marahau reminded me of a scene in the British film *Chariots of Fire*. I absolutely loved kayaking with the two-to-four-week-old seal pups out in the ocean. Sea kayaking the route instead of tramping is really a wonderful opportunity, as the Abel Tasman National Park looks even more beautiful from the water.

Since 1998, I am happy to report, there have been amazing partnerships formed between the Department of Conservation and local people to control the pests in the area and to monitor kiwi. The most recent of these is Project Janszoon, founded in 2012 and named after Abel Tasman's patronymic middle name. Project Janszoon is described on its website as a thirty-year project which will run until the four hundredth anniversary of Tasman's sighting of New Zealand, which will arrive in 2042.[61] Members of the community have been given kiwi monitors, and the Department of Conservation in Nelson also receives money from wealthy Aucklanders more informally. It is the only growing DOC branch in the country, with significant private funding and local participation. These days the native species have come back, and things have definitely changed for the better.

Finally, I should add that this area is not far from the ecologically significant Farewell Spit – also worth a visit.

CHAPTER TWENTY

Honeymoon on the Heaphy Track

FROM GOLDEN BAY TO PALMS AND PENGUINS

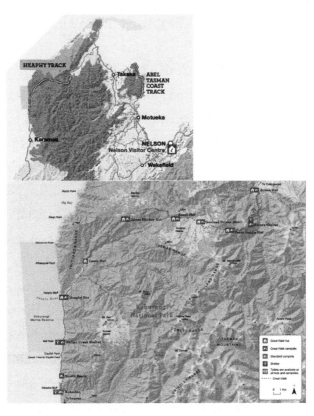

Heaphy Track. From *Heathy Track* (brochure),
Wellington, Department of Conservation, September 2016

223

I HAVE tramped the Heaphy Track, another one of New Zealand's Great Walks, twice, first completing it in December 1998 – so I have really been involved in trekking for some time! The walk stretches through the Kahurangi National Park at the top of the South Island, west of the famous Abel Tasman Track, and winds its way through native bush and tussock downs to the wild Pacific Ocean on the West Coast. The track can be walked in either direction, beginning at the eastern end at Brown Hut, or starting in Karamea on the West Coast by driving fifteen kilometres north to the Kohaihai River campsite.

Named after the early New Zealand explorer Charles Heaphy who was the first to traverse the coastal portion of the trail, the Heaphy Track is believed to have first been explored by Māori who settled by the river in the thirteenth and fourteenth centuries. Although named after Heaphy, it was fellow explorer James Mackay who, with two others, first blazed the full route in 1862, beginning the development of the Track.[62] Nowadays, the track is one of the most popular in the series of New Zealand's Great Walks being walked or mountain biked in 2013 by over six thousand people.[63]

On my first tramp of the Heaphy in 1998, I caught the local shuttle bus to Collingwood where I was to begin my tramp. After catching a lift to Brown Hut, to which the bus now runs, I began hiking the seventeen and a half kilometres uphill towards Perry Saddle Hut, which took about five hours. It was a very hot and dry summer and I was drinking bottle after bottle of water. On the track, I met an Israeli girl who had just left the Israeli Army and was traumatised from her experience. She had only been in the country for two months and was telling me about a Palestinian guy she had been going out with while she was still in the army. She said someone might have shot her if they found out, and I remember thinking, 'Goodness, we don't know how lucky we are in this country!'

I also met another couple from Auckland who had been really looking forward to tramping the Heaphy Track. They told me they had been training to do the Heaphy by running around the block with heavy chains wrapped around their bodies for extra weight!

As in some other parts of the book, the photographs in this section have been kindly passed on to me by Nicki Botica Williams, a very able photographer. Nicki and her husband Kevin took the photographs in this section while on their recent honeymoon. It might have been perfect, except for the fact that the huts were quite busy with other people.

Back in 1998, my party and I made it to Perry Saddle Hut and spent the night there before tramping onwards for six and a half hours through tussock clearings and beech trees towards James Mackay Hut. At a bit over twenty-four kilometres, this was the longest stretch of the track, but I passed a lot of interesting sights along the way, including the famous pole from which trampers have been hanging their old boots for years. From James Mackay

Bring a tent on a busy walk like the Heaphy: you will have more privacy!

225

Hut, I began a six-hour walk of a bit over twenty kilometres to Heaphy Hut. Along the way, you have to cross a new bridge over the Heaphy River.

In those days, before the Heaphy became a Great Walk, they used to have walkwires where one wire would be at feet level and you put your arm up and hold onto the higher wire. That was pretty rough, I thought. So, I'm glad they've now been replaced by a proper swing bridge. Still, it was a great walk in more ways than one even then, and I loved the nīkau palms along this section of the track because they reminded me of the west coast of Auckland.

I spent the night in Heaphy Hut where I discovered the infamous West Coast mosquitoes. I found out that they can get into your sleeping bag even if you've got the hood over your head and the string tied up at the top, when one snuck in at 6.00 am and woke me up. I couldn't believe it! On a previous occasion, I've been to the beach at Jackson Bay, which is further down the West Coast, and the mosquitoes there came up under my t-shirt.

The final stretch of the tramp took me just over sixteen kilometres along the beautiful, yet rugged, coastline of the West Coast to the Kohaihai River mouth, a lovely five-hour walk to conclude what had been an incredible tramp. A profusion of nikau, the world's most southerly variety of palm tree, growing out of white sand make this area resemble part of an island in the South Pacific – but wait, it is part of an island in the South Pacific!

And yet at the same time, if you are lucky, you might see penguins on the beach. The west coast of the South Island is one of the few places where you will see palm trees and penguins together in the wild.

The Heaphy Track: mountains, bush, and the sea at either end

Nicki and Kevin at Flanagans Corner, the highest point on the Heaphy Track

*Close-ups of nature on
the Heaphy Track*

A bridge typical of the more popular New Zealand tracks: in the real back-country there are sometimes only wires for hands and feet ('walkwires')

An ancient snail from when New Zealand was part of Gondwanaland

Palm trees and penguins at the West Coast end, side by side

CHAPTER TWENTY-ONE

The Nelson Lakes, the Travers Range and the Travers-Sabine Circuit

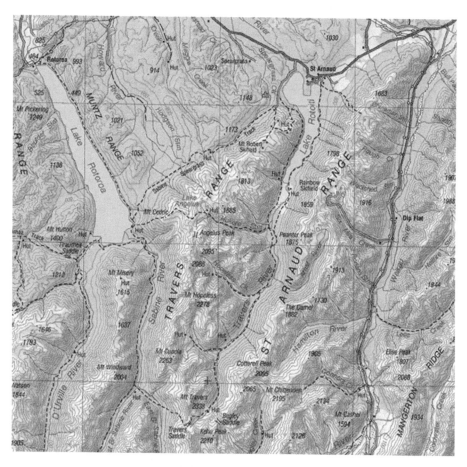

*The Nelson Lakes, Travers Range, and the
Travers River-Sabine River Circuit.*

Imagery from LINZ via NZTopomaps.com

I N 2013 I had made it my goal to climb Mont Blanc in France and was intending to climb Mount Aspiring in New Zealand afterwards if I was successful. As part of my training, I wanted to tramp to the Angelus Hut and around the Travers-Sabine Circuit in the Nelson Lakes National Park area, so I invited my friend James from Ireland to come to New Zealand to go tramping with me. I had seen him in New Zealand over many periods of my life and he had stayed at my place in Auckland twice. I had met him in the USA and we had travelled from Los Angeles to Las Vegas and had a great time there. We had met a woman with a red convertible who had just got out of rehab and she showed us Las Vegas in one night – after that crazy experience we had become very good friends.

James had been white-water kayaking all over the world, from the UK to North and South America, and had even kayaked parts of Africa. He was now running a business selling gluten-free sauces and other products, but still looked really fit in his photos when we had made contact again on Facebook. I told him about my training and how we would be camping out in the Nelson Lakes area, and then gave him some simple instructions to make sure he knew how to put up and take down his tent and to bring boots which he had previously worn.

When James arrived, it turned out that he had gained some weight and looked unfit. But we stuck to the plan and drove towards Nelson. I went shopping for all of our food and showed him how to pack a tramping pack, then we stayed the night in Kaikoura in my tent because he hadn't learnt how to set his tent up. So, on night one, he was out reading the instructions for it with a torch! In retrospect, I shouldn't have gone through with the tramp, but at the time we had decided to carry on. We drove to the village of St Arnaud on the edge of Lake Rotoiti and camped out beside the lake, looking out at the low-lying clouds around the lake. While at St Arnaud, I decided to hire a locator beacon, more for James' safety than my own.

The eighty-kilometre Travers-Sabine Circuit that we were tramping usually takes four to seven days to complete. However, I planned to shorten it to less than seventy kilometres by tramping to Angelus Hut and then cutting across to join the circuit. We had views of the plains and both sides of the ridge as we ascended. This scenic walk reaches deep into the mountainous land surrounding Lake Rotoiti and Lake Rotoroa, which are themselves only a one-and-a-half-hour drive inland from Nelson. These lakes were once important for Māori travelling to and from to the places where the precious pounamu (greenstone) was quarried, as they provided a plentiful source of food. However, it was for their incredible scenic value that the Nelson Lakes were gazetted as a national park in 1956.

We took the Robert Ridge Route up the northern half of the Robert Range to Lake Angelus, a route which was reportedly first climbed in 1860. As outdoor explorers began to frequent the area soon after, the small alpine lake known to Māori as Rotomaninitua. In this context, roto means lake, manini means pleasant, and tua means isolated and high-up: altogether an excellent description. The lake was then named Rangimārie, a Māori word meaning quiet or peaceful, a name that in a curious quirk of history was actually bestowed upon it by Pākehā mountain-climbers unaware that it had a name among local Māori already (South Island Māori populations were sparse compared to the North Island and Rotomaninitua, isolated and high-up, was presumably not the site of a permanent habitation). The lake was soon renamed Angelus, along with a nearby peak of the same name, after a devotional prayer inspired by its Pākehā-Māori name. These days the lake is officially Rotomaninitua / Lake Angelus.

The Robert Ridge Route is accessed initially by the Pinchgut Track, which doesn't sound very inviting and is very steep and winding. The Pinchgut takes climbers up to the treeline, which as we recall is quite low in New Zealand. The route flattens out after that, along an open, exposed tundra ridge with poles for guidance: no use in fog! The poled route eventually climbs to a maximum elevation of 1,794 metres above sea level at the Julius Summit, or approximately six thousand feet. This is an altitude which does not sound like much by the standards of the Himalayas, or the Rockies – about the same as Denver – but which is in fact totally alpine even in the comparatively warm Nelson region and not for beginners or the unprepared, even in summer. The route then descends slightly to the hut, which stands at 1,650 metres above sea level.

Lake Angelus was mesmerising and had shiny waters surrounded by snow when we were there. By the way we were tramping in summer, in December to be precise. That's what I mean about totally alpine.

In fact, for reasons I've explained above, the sight of snow in summer is fairly common in the South Island, even in places that aren't actually alpine. A friend reminds me of sitting on a beach on Lake Manapouri, several hundred kilometres south of Nelson, around New Year's Day, when people were sunbathing in skimpy costumes, and looking out over the dappled waters to a shady south-facing hillside above the lake but not that far above, where there sat a great patch of snow! Obviously, it didn't get much sun there. But it was still a surprise to see something like that lingering well into summer at an altitude that was only a few hundred metres above sea level.

In the vicinity of Lake Manapouri at that time we were wearing puffy cold-weather gear quite often, putting it on whenever the sun went behind a cloud. So much for the often surprisingly anaemic New Zealand summer, which has something of a British quality even though New Zealand is much closer to the equator, with clearer air, stronger sunlight and shorter 'burn times'.

As in Britain, the New Zealand summer has a quality of blowing hot one day and cold the next, a changeable quality which the sight of palm trees on the beach can belie.

It's fair to say that there are no palm trees anywhere near Lake Manapouri! But even in the literally palmier parts of the country, the weather is often unseasonal. And this is especially true in the mountains.

As we left the Mt Robert carpark near Lake Rotoiti to ascend the Pinchgut, James kept asking if we were really going up that high, but I just completely ignored it. It was not an easy hike and on the way up he got very puffed and said he felt as if his back was collapsing. Then he told me his back had been broken in a white-water rafting contest and I wasn't very happy with him only telling me that halfway up.

The route we had taken followed a broad ridge to Julius Summit and then we went onto a sharp and rocky section of the track. There was a lot of volcanic rock and we also went through snow where we definitely needed the poles that marked the track. It was a nice day and we were very lucky to have great weather and not too much wind along Robert Ridge. Still, the more than twelve kilometres uphill from the car park to Julius Summit was slow going. It should have taken us about six hours, but we started at nine a.m. and arrived at Angelus Hut at five p.m., so it had taken us eight hours.

The hut, which is nestled in alongside Lake Angelus, requires booking if you are going to use the bunks. There was an Ultimate Hikes group there whose two guides were making dinner for the people in the hut when we arrived. Ultimate Hikes is an organisation that generally runs tramps all around the country where people take their own packs along. Many of the people in that group were fit enough to do their own tramping, they just wanted to be guided. So, while they had dinner on tablecloths, I started talking to a DOC ranger named who told me that she had just resigned because she had had enough of the people who were staying and was more interested in doing research on rock wrens.

I had an interesting time at Angelus Hut, but we were in tents and it was quite cold. The speargrass we had pitched our tents on was wet, so I was quite angry about that at the time. The Robert Ridge Route to Angelus Hut was not the only route back to our carpark; there is also a route called the Speargrass Route that descends rapidly to the treeline and runs below the treeline after that. The Roberts Ridge Route is mostly on the tops; the Speargrass Route is mostly in the bush and is often used in bad weather. James and I got in a row and I told him he should go down by way of the Speargrass Route, and then he could hang around the Cascade Track and maybe go to the Lakehead Hut above Lake Rotoiti, because I was going to carry on with the Travers-Sabine Circuit. I was so furious that I left him behind at Lake Angelus, after giving him the beacon and showing him how to use it.

By the way, it's extra-important to fill in hut intention books and to have beacons and good communications and all the gear, and to stick to tracks that have lots of people coming and going, and safe routes for the less fit such as the Speargrass, if you are going to split up like this (and even then, I would not recommend it). In the old days, the rule of thumb was that four was the minimum safe party size, but that was in the days when things were possibly a bit more basic than they are today (no GPS for one thing).

Above all, it is good advice not to step off the track, nor to get lost in fog on a poled route and stupidly wander away from it. Even in places that aren't far from a modern city you can get into a genuine survival epic, really quick, if that happens. Nor is it a good idea to split up if there will be any river crossings involved, of the sort where somebody might get knocked out on the rocks or otherwise need support or rescue, and where there is no bridge available to make a dry crossing.

(Although people think of New Zealand as a verdant paradise with none of the sinister connotations of those dry, flat parts of Australia "where the dead men lie" as a famous Aussie poem from the 1890s has it, outdoor New Zealand is probably the more dangerous place, at least as far as natural hazards go. Though the inhabitants of the Australian mainland face thirst and heat and a greater variety of things that have some kind of deadly bite, on the other hand, in the flat terrain typical of most of Australia the only fall you need fear is falling on your face and there is less chance of routinely encountering a swift river than in New Zealand. And there is probably less chance of freezing to death as well.)

To all that I might add that if there are no surprises in the fitness department, you probably won't feel the need to risk splitting up in the first place. Along with the other aspects of preparation, such as telling people where you are going and when you expect to be back, making sure that there are no major differences in fitness among the members of the group is an important aspect of getting ready to go into the New Zealand outdoors, and one that is often overlooked.

Having thus made the possibly ill-advised decision to split up, though I had made sure to send James back by the safer route with the beacon, I headed towards John Tait Hut in the Travers Valley, following the Hukere Stream downhill for about four hours to the Cascade Track Junction, where it was a further two to three hours to reach John Tait Hut.

Along the way, I met the ranger I had seen earlier, who was out doing research on the rock wren in the Travers Valley. She had seen one the day before and was trying to see if it was still there. I started talking to her about the study she was helping to conduct and she said that the rock wren was becoming an endangered species. There was only one left in the valley. And there were not many kea either: a wild species which seems more numerous than it really is because of a pigeon-like habit of hanging around campgrounds and carparks in the hope of freebies. The kea you see in such places might very well be a significant proportion of the total.

The views in this stretch of the track leading to John Tait Hut were just spot on, with the volcanic rock making for a beautiful subalpine environment. I camped out here underneath Mt Travers and the following morning followed the track up over the Travers Saddle (1,787m) to West Sabine Hut, which was a long walk normally taking about nine to twelve hours. The track passes through the Cupola Creek chasm and climbs steeply up a gorge then eases off into forest and tussock land before reaching Upper Travers Hut. From there the track steepens considerably towards the alpine pass of the Saddle, before dropping sharply through tussock, scree and beech forests to West Sabine Hut, which is 1,107m below the saddle.

From there I made it up to Rotomairewhenua / Blue Lake, a small lake with incredibly pristine waters at an elevation of 1,200m above sea level.

Goodness knows how he did it, but James managed to catch up with me at the West Sabine Hut. He had told everyone at the hut how I had abandoned him, so when I turned up after climbing over the Travers Saddle, everyone looked at me like I was some kind of monster and he went away and hid. The hut was full, with about thirty people, so I pitched my tent outside and went back in to grab one of the cushions out of the hut so I could have a comfortable sleep. James came out behind me and said hello, and I told him I couldn't believe he'd made it to the hut! He begged me to allow him to spend one more night in the national park, so I agreed to

Camping by Lake Rotoiti

*Snow Tramping on
the Robert Ridge*

Lake Angelus

Lake Angelus

DOC Ranger looking
at Rock Wren

Upper Travers Hut

The Travers Saddle

Lake Rotoroa

Blue Lake

Chamoix

spend one night at Speargrass Hut on my way out, while he caught me up. It was a very safe route from this point back to the Mount Robert carpark.

From West Sabine Hut, it's a five-hour walk through the valley following the river to the Sabine Hut and its wide views of Lake Rotoroa, and then another five hours up towards Speargrass Hut through a series of small valleys and wetlands. It was quite a long walk and halfway along the track I realised I didn't have any food left because I had been planning to walk out that day. All I had left was a muesli bar and no dinner to look forward to at the hut.

I met an American guy along the way and talking to him made me realise it's unbelievable what people tell you when you go tramping! When I did Makarora, near Wanaka, there were some trampers who had had a death in the family, and on top of the Wilkin/Young Track there were two people who had recently divorced – but this American topped them all. He was around 40 years old and said he had been active for most of his life, although he had had to have hip replacements because he was a skateboarder in his 20s and 30s and injured himself, I suppose. That was interesting enough, but the story gets worse: he told me he was a drug mule coming to New Zealand to bring loads of cocaine in. I don't know why he wanted to tell me this, but I didn't really appreciate the information! He also wanted a wife, and then proceeded to ask me if I needed $20,000, so I turned around and told him I didn't need nor want that kind of money.

When I got to Speargrass Hut, I was ravenous. Apart from a sachet of soup which the guy from the States had given me (and it did turn out to be soup), there wasn't a crumb of food left in my backpack. There was a hunter there who had just caught a chamois, a type of wild goat or antelope that like so many other four-footed mammals had been introduced to New Zealand by early settlers. He had its carcass hanging on a hook. I looked at it, and said, 'Oh, for goodness sake, can I please have a bite?' The hunter said, 'Look, it's not very good fresh.' I knew that because as with the venison that I buy, chamois is only good meat if it's aged. Still, I begged him to give me a chunk, so he cut off a piece the size of the palm of my hand and gave it to me. I had no cooking oil so I boiled it and it was rock-hard, but I chewed on it anyway because I was that hungry. Honestly, the three-hour walk to the Mount Robert car park the next day could not go quickly enough and getting out and finally meeting up again with James was even better, as I could finally get some real food!

CHAPTER TWENTY-TWO
Cobb Valley, Mount Arthur and the Nelson Tablelands

I
N my first book, *A Maverick Traveller*, I wrote about trips to the Cobb Valley and Kahurangi National Park, I didn't include photographs of those places. Following a brief overview of the area, I include some photographs here.

Kahurangi National Park is the second largest national park in New Zealand after Fiordland. With over five hundred and seventy kilometres of tracks, including the famous seventy-eight kilometre Heaphy Track, Kahurangi is tramping heaven. With its coastal palm forests, marble mountains, rare birds like the rock wren and the spotted kiwi, and tussock high country, it's an incredible place to be.

In Māori Kahurangi means treasured possession, which is exactly what this park is. For hundreds of years the Māori used tracks through this region to find greenstone, called pounamu in Māori, which they used for prized jewellery passed down from one generation to the next.

Part of the Kahurangi National Park, the Cobb Valley can be accessed from the Upper Takaka district, at the base of the Takaka Hill along thirty-eight kilometres of unsealed road. Mount Arthur, the principal mountain in the area, can be reached via the Graham Valley Road, thirty-five kilometres from Motueka. Access to the Nelson Tablelands, a high plateau, can be gained on foot via each of these two routes, and the west coast of the South Island can be reached from the Leslie-Karamea Track.

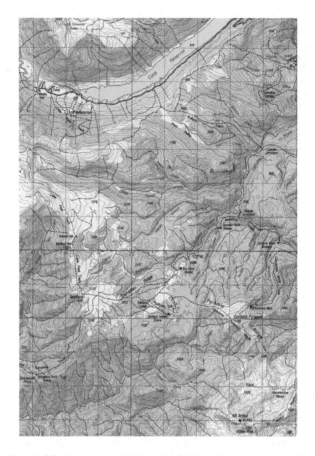

The Cobb Reservoir, Nelson Tablelands, Mount Arthur and Asbestos Cottage. (LINZ via NZTopomaps.com, 2017)

The diverse terrain I covered included a series of unique geological features. Mt Arthur is made of hard, crystalline marble: below the ground are some of the deepest shafts and most intricate cave systems in the world. Cavers have currently joined two cave systems in the area and made a massive thirty-six kilometres long, twelve hundred metres deep underground labyrinth. Nettlebed is now the deepest cave in the Southern Hemisphere of which the depth is known.

Cobb Reservoir (above), nominally 819 metres above sea level on the surface. The tops above the reservoir are as high up again, and it is at that point that the Nelson Tablelands are reached. The images below show Balloon Hut in the Tablelands not far south of Cobb Reservoir, reached after a steep climb, and a general view of the Tablelands.

In contrast, the Tablelands are made of limestone and quartz that were lifted and twisted over millennia to form mountains. The Cobb Valley is different again: its rivers were once glaciers smoothing and polishing the rock as they advanced to form a U-shaped valley, always the sign of a now-vanished glacier as opposed to the steep V that is carved by a river. The valley today still bears many signs of its former glaciers and is filled with volcanic rock, schist and sandstone.

The picturesque Lower Gridiron Shelter

The Upper Gridiron Hut, built into an immense rock overhang.

Flora Hut, another of the unique huts in this area (middle);
Asbestos Cottage (bottom)

249

*Another view of the Asbestos Cottage exterior and
two views of the inside of the cottage*

The sign in the photograph above points to a feature called Gordons Pyramid (below), near Mount Arthur (bottom, with low cloud)

251

Vegetable Sheep or Cushion Plant, Raoulia *species*

View from the Top of Mount Arthur on a better day

Ridge and Scree

Slow going up a scree slope

CHAPTER TWENTY-THREE

St James Walkway and the Lewis Pass Tops

MOUNTAINS, RIVERS, AND OLD HUTS

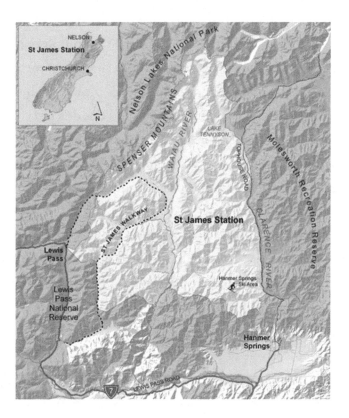

St James Station, after which the St James Walkway was named, was acquired by the New Zealand Government in 2008 and incorporated into a wider St James Conservation Area. The Lewis Pass Tops are just on the other side of State Highway 7, in Lewis Pass National Reserve.

(DOC graphics, from press release 'St James Station', 8 October 2008, at https://www.beehive.govt.nz/node/34954

253

THE St James Walkway is named after the former St James Station upon which most of the walkway's sixty-six kilometres is located. In the map on the preceding page, the station is shown as brown while the surrounding area is green; this is purely a convention reflecting land use zoning, and much of the St James Station was, and remains, a wilderness similar to the surrounding nature reserves.

The St James was a sheep station, meaning ranch, which was acquired by the New Zealand Government for conservation purposes in 2008, the bottom having fallen out of New Zealand sheep farming a generation earlier. There used to be seventy million sheep in New Zealand a bit over thirty years ago. Now there are only thirty million, and this downturn presumably rendered places like St James somewhat marginal. The station was rebadged as the St James Conservation Area. Having said that the St James Walkway had long been in existence, courtesy of a kindly owner one presumes, even when the area was a ranch.

By New Zealand standards the St James Walkway is a comparatively easy tramp, though there is a lot of exposure to Alpine weather. Most of the distance is tramped on river flats, but nowhere is below five hundred metres of elevation and the highest point, the Anne Saddle, is over eleven hundred metres up. There are eight huts along the way.

The St James is in one of my favourite parts of New Zealand, the Lewis Pass / Muruia Valley area in the middle of the northern half of the Southern Alps, more or less due west of Kaikoura. The St James Walkway is reached by means of State Highway 7, which zigzags through the area.

There are numerous other tramps off to the side of State Highway 7 in the Lewis Pass / Maruia Valley area, such as the Lake Daniell (formerly lake Daniells) tramp, Lake Christabel, the Lewis Tops Track, and others.

And there are hot pools at Maruia (commercial) and at Sylvia Flats (do-it-yourself).

The Maruia Valley is also famous as the place where a key document of the modern conservation era, the Maruia Declaration, was first signed in 1975. Circulated as an ultimately successful petition against the logging of native forests, it gained 340,000 signatures by 1977, which at the time meant that over one New Zealander in ten signed it and a still higher proportion of adults.

Last day, sore feet

Day one in the bus known as Big Blue

Day one, too wet

Lake Daniell – what it's all about

St James Walkway Scenes

St James Walkway Scenes

258

*Standing in front of one of the several rivers that
the St James Walkway follows*

Lewis Pass Tops with Alpine Flora

One of two varieties of Tikumu, or Mountain Daisy (left); One of several species of Speargrass, which also goes by other names (right)

CHAPTER TWENTY-FOUR

Welcome Flat

THE BEST HOT POOLS

The Route to Welcome Flat from the Haast Highway.

From Copland Track to Welcome Flat Hut (brochure), Franz
Josef Glacier, Department of Conservation, October 2016

As attractive as the tramping and hot pools around the Lewis Pass and Maruia Valley are, my favourite tramping-track hot pools are to be found further south, at Welcome Flat. Welcome Flat is on the Copland River, a tributary of the Karangarua River which runs from the Southern Alps down to the Tasman Sea at a location south of Fox Glacier. Welcome Flat is on the lower part of the Copland River, at an altitude of about 430 metres, with a very flash hut. Further east you come to the much more mundane Douglas Rock Hut, surrounded by giant mountains. Douglas Rock Hut gives people a taste of being in the Southern Alps without having to do serious climbing. But it is serious thereafter. The track terminates at an altitude of 2,150 metres at the Copland Pass, by which stage you are halfway up Mount Cook.

Welcome Flat Hot Pools, Sierra Range in background (above).
Kea playing (below).

Way in from west

View past Welcome Flat to the mountains

Douglas Rock Hut and environs

CHAPTER TWENTY-FIVE

Towns, Traditions and Gardens

— a special section written by Chris Harris

A LTHOUGH people tend to think of New Zealand as a rural or farming nation – rugby, racing and beer, as they used to say – and even today as an essentially outdoor playground, it shouldn't be overlooked that the country also has an urban or urbane side. Most New Zealanders have lived in towns or cities since the early 1900s, and even in the nineteenth century a sizeable minority lived in cities. According to a classic essay published in the 1950s, it was already the case that by 1881, "Dunedin had emerged . . . to become a 'handsome city' of over 40,000 people. . . . its twenty-two miles of streets were paved and well lighted. Fine buildings of Oamaru limestone or local basalt lined its main thoroughfares. . . . and it was the site of the four and five storied headquarters of the colony's leading manufacturing concerns and business houses."[64]

In fact, the early settlers, who were mostly British-born and had mostly come out to New Zealand as adults, and thus carried British cultural attitudes with them, were anxious that New Zealand should be made as similar to Britain as possible, with towns and cities to match.

In the South Island, where settlement developed most rapidly in the mid-nineteenth century, an effort was made to achieve an ancient look by means of Georgian, neoclassical and gothic architecture, and by building in stone to the greatest extent possible. So effective was this effort that the French visitor Andre Siegfried wrote that Christchurch had already, by 1904, "an ancient air . . . the strange, tranquil and respectable appearance of an old European city."[65]

Some of the results can be seen in the following historical photographs, in chronological order. Nor were parks and gardens neglected. As mentioned in *A Maverick Traveller*, the settlers were very keen on planting deciduous trees and colourful flowers, both somewhat lacking in New Zealand. In fact, a striking characteristic of was the creation of large, encompassing 'town belts' as they are known in New Zealand, great parks that have a linear form and surround the downtown area, as they do in the Australian city of Adelaide as well. In practice these town belts usually contain a mixture of native bush – disliked in quantity, but of which remnants were often saved – European-style trees and flowers, sportsfields, and open parkland.

'Strange, Tranquil and Respectable' Christchurch. View of Canterbury College, Worcester St and Canterbury Museum, Rolleston Street.

Ref: 1/2-055425-F. Alexander Turnbull Library, Wellington, New Zealand.
http://natlib.govt.nz/records/22917645

*The Crescent, Invercargill, from Tay Street circa 1905, by Muir &
Moodie Studio. The internationally popular Invercargill March was
composed around this time by local boy Alex Lithgow.*

Soutce: Te Papa (C.012926). http://collections.tepapa.govt.nz/
Object/19511. Empty sky cropped.

Christchurch, known as New Zealand's 'garden city', lost its town belt
to development – but only because the embankment of the Avon River and
the enormous Hagley Park were together considered adequate in any case.

In 1958, New Zealand was visited by Nikolaus Pevsner, the former editor
of London's *Architectural Review*. In a transcript of a radio talk published
in the *New Zealand Listener* on 12 December 1958 under the title 'Towns
and Traditions', Pevsner wrote that "The University [Arts Centre] and the
Museum at Christchurch – these are very typical examples of the official
architecture of the High Victorian moment in New Zealand. I need not tell
you how admirable was the confidence and the ambitiousness to erect such
buildings in the sixties and seventies [of the 1800s] in towns still of a tiny
size. They are of course Gothic and they are of the local stones of the South

Dunedin: The Octagon, November 1949. This is a precinct closely modelled on Moray Place in the New Town of Edinburgh.

Source: Dunedin. Whites Aviation Ltd: Photographs. Ref: WA-23421-G. Alexander Turnbull Library, Wellington, New Zealand.

Canterbury Provincial Council Chamber (Great Hall). This was highly decorated in colours of red and gold, as is shown online in colour images on Te Ara. The source for the 1920s view shown here is Christchurch City Libraries, Photo CD17, Img 0012.

Dunedin, showing Town Belt and City Centre. (Google Earth/ Satellite, imagery ©CNES/ Astrium, Cnes/SpotImage, DigitalGlobe, map data ©2016 Google).

Invercargill, showing Town Belt and Queen's Park. (Google Earth/Satellite, imagery ©CNES/Astrium, Cnes/SpotImage, DigitalGlobe, Map Data ©2016 Google.)

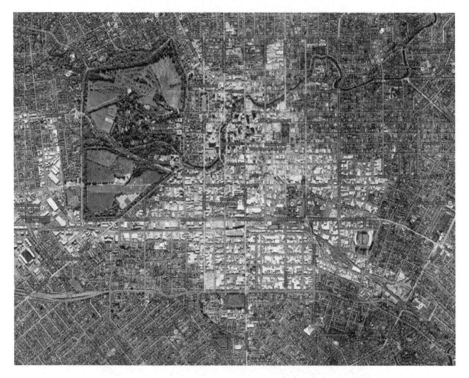

Christchurch Central Area. (Google Earth/Satellite, imagery ©2016
CNES/Astrium, Cnes/SpotImage, DigitalGlobe. Map data ©2016 Google)

Island. Here again Christchurch and Dunedin read as against Wellington and Auckland."

Another writer with an architectural bent, Walter Benjamin, famously described Paris as "the capital of the nineteenth century." Behind Benjamin's quip lay the fact that much of what we consider to be distinctive about Paris is the product of nineteenth-century rebuilding efforts, from the Arc de Triomphe to the Champs-Elysee to the Eiffel Tower to the distinctive form of Second Empire architecture with its mansard roofs.

If the observations of Pevsner and Benjamin are read one after the other, it becomes clear that if the nineteenth century gave us Paris, it also laid a heavy imprint upon Christchurch and Dunedin and the lesser centres of the South Island, which were indeed contemporary with Paris. In his 2008 book *The Life and Times of Auckland*, Gordon McLauchlan wrote that Auckland should not be looked down on as a young city, "because almost all cities are young."[66] In other words our urban heritage is just as significant as that of Europe and comes from the same culture, admittedly at a distance. We can't just say, 'oh that's all just colonial stuff, let's bowl it and move on'. Touring Europe before the 2011 earthquake I would pass through the sorts of old European Cities that André Siegfried described Christchurch as resembling, and I would think, 'gosh, this place is just like Christchurch'.

Pevsner added that "The quality of the main buildings in the four towns," that is to say of Auckland, Wellington Christchurch and Dunedin, "varies greatly. Some . . . might stand in any much larger town in England, for example the provincial Council Chamber at Christchurch designed in the mid-sixties, the [Anglican] Cathedral of Christchurch designed in 1864 by the most successful English architect of the period, Sir George Gilbert Scott; or St. Matthews at Auckland by Pearson, the architect of Truro Cathedral and one of the most serious and sensitive of English late Gothicists; or the Theomin residence at Dunedin by Sir Ernest George, one of the two internationally influential domestic architects of the late Victorian decades." St. Matthews is a rare example of a stone building in Auckland and of absolutely striking quality. Unfortunately, it is hemmed in by tall, ugly buildings of more recent construction, including a car parking building right next door, and thus somewhat hidden away.

A seeming indifference to heritage issues in more recent times, an indifference which became very obvious in the context of the official response to the Christchurch or Canterbury earthquakes that reached their crescendo of destructiveness in February 2011 – Canterbury is the wider region, and many country towns and historic homesteads were damaged in addition to Christchurch – brings me to the fact that the early urban culture of New Zealand has often been erased and forgotten in a manner analogous to the physical bulldozing of older buildings: a process of forgetting that the rural / farming legend has tended to foster.

Though cloaked in rural mythology, this legend has often served as a pretext for various forms of urban philistinism such as that of the fast-buck school of developers, or of promoters of motorways and big roads in sensitive urban areas. How better to ensure that nobody notices or complains when urban heritage is lost than by insisting that the 'real' New Zealand is to be found outside city limits, to the actual exclusion of any kind of urban culture whatsoever?

This problem of a waning of urban culture has had its greatest impact on the North Island, where urban growth has mostly taken place later than in the South, under the control of the New Zealand-born rather than that of British-born colonists among whom the urban culture was still strong.

Leaving the South behind now, the great tragedy of urbanisation in the North Island and of Auckland in particular is that the high degree of intelligence applied to the early planning of the cities of the South Island by British colonists was not extended to the North as the cities there expanded under the supervision of locally-born New Zealanders who were used to thinking of their country as rural and did not see why sensitive forms of town planning or urban design needed to be practiced here. Thus, the opportunity to create a magnificent modern city in Auckland as that city grew from a quarter of a million inhabitants in 1945 to more than 1.5 million today, was lost.

For instance, Auckland had a rough equivalent to the town belts of Invercargill and Dunedin in the form of a system of gullies that led from

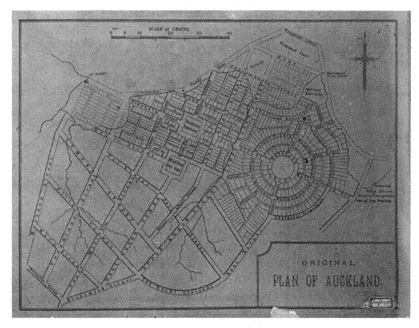

*Felton Mathew's 1841 plan for Auckland as subsequently
redrawn for early twentieth century re-publication.*
Auckland Libraries reference NZ Map 2664.

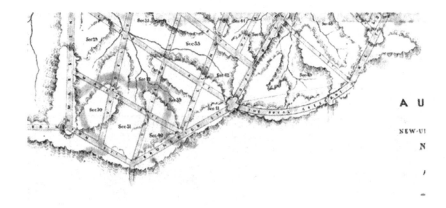

*Detail of stately streets and crescents overlooking gully
system from Mathew's original plan.* Auckland Libraries
reference NZ Map 6631, Sir George Grey Special Collections.

Western Springs to the west of the downtown, to the Auckland Domain to the east of the downtown. These gullies, respectively Kingsland Gully, Arch Hill Gully, Newton Gully and Grafton Gully, were never fully built upon because they were too damp and low-lying. An early plan for Auckland did actually propose that the gullies be treated as town belts. The government surveyor Felton Mathew's plan of 1840, shown on the preceding page, proposed a series of crescents along the edges of the gullies, crescents along which terraces of townhouses would be built to overlook the gullies: "Guided by this principle, I have in several instances, adopted the Crescent form, as one to which the ground is peculiarly adapted: indeed, it could not be made available in any other shape," wrote Mathew.[67]

The gullies survived for a long time. Grafton Gully was described in 1930 "a beautiful scenic reserve of native bush in the heart of the city," (*Auckland: The Gateway to New Zealand*, 1930) and "a delightful reserve of bush," within which "nothing could be more pleasant than to wander here on a summer's day–along paths cool and flecked with leafy light and shadow." (*Auckland: City of Sunshine*, 1942). All the same they were taken for the motorways in the late 1960s and in the 1970s.

And so, St. Matthews in Auckland is today overshadowed by awful architectural tat, including the Casino. There is no trace of the awareness of the importance of what Pevsner called "visual planning," of a city pleasing to the eye, nor indeed of any other sort of planning, such as the healthy influence of town belts and fine, walkable grids of streets. Auckland is full of unhealthy people who spend two hours a day in a traffic jam.

CHAPTER TWENTY-SIX
Queenstown's Welcome Cove

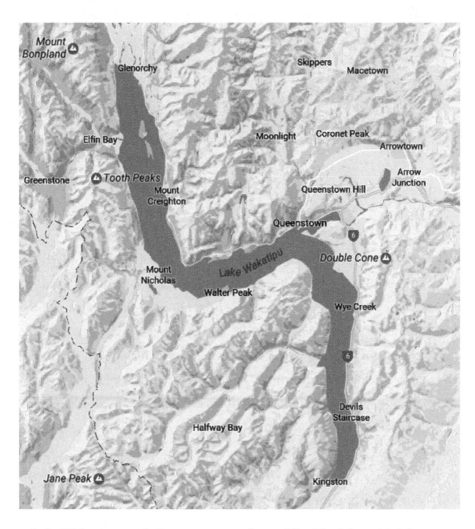

Lake Wakatipu, with Queenstown in the middle. The lake is 80 kilometres long and up to 380 metres deep. Map data ©2017 Google.

Queenstown, from Bob's Peak on Ben Lomond.

By Lawrence Murray, CC BY 2.0, https://commons.
wikimedia.org/w/index.php?curid=37661081n

As a result, people flee Auckland in pursuit of healthier lifestyles. Queenstown, where I live, has accessible walks near the city and the only reason I go to the gym is because of the hot pools that are part of the gym complex. Queenstown appears to be a very fit city, as you see people both running and biking in the snow here. The Ben Lomond mountain track is an eight-hour return trip, or six-hour return if you take the gondola, while around Queenstown Hill and Arrowtown there are many other walks.

In contrast to most Otago place-names, Queenstown is neither Scottish nor Māori but the Victorian-era name for the city now known as Cobh in the Republic of Ireland. Cobh is pronounced 'Cove' and is an Irish borrowing of the English word 'Cove', a still earlier name for the town. The original Cove/Queenstown had several claims to fame, often tragic. It was the last departure point of 2.5 million Irish bound for the New World, and of the *Titanic*. During the First World War, heavily armed British warships disguised as easy commercial prey would also set out from Queenstown in Ireland to tempt U-boats to attack them, ships known as Q-Ships: a secret spy theme taken up in the 1930s thriller *Q-Planes*.

Amid the violence of post-World War One revolution and a sudden upsurge of nationalism, Queenstown became Cobh.

Our Queenstown, of which the original Māori name for the locality, Tāhuna, refers to coastal shallows, is also located on a cove of Lake Wakatipu and this is probably a factor in its acquisition of same name as the Irish town. But there the resemblance ends, for the South Island's Queenstown does not have such a dramatic history. It is just a tourist resort on the big lake Wakatipu, up and down which the TSS or twin-screw steamer Earnslaw plies. Once an ocean-going vessel, the Earnslaw was broken down and crated up by its owners to Lake Wakatipu more than a hundred years ago, in the belief that that would be more profitable, and has puffed up and down the lake ever since, strangely captive like a toad in a hole.

Irish postage stamp commemorating 25th anniversary of the 1916 Easter Rising, 1941. Source: Internet thumbnail.

TSS Earnslaw
in harbour,
Queenstown

Some English
visitors loving it,
on Ben Lomond
above Queenstown

Another view
from Ben
Lomond

Still, Queenstown on Lake Wakatipu has its own history, a great multicultural one, as the Chinese formed two-thirds of the gold mining workforce here in the 1860s. In the Arrowtown Museum, it states that the Chinese goldminers, who preferred opium over alcohol, were never raucous or violent like other miners.

Like many small cities that are handy to bigger ones, Queenstown has the best of both worlds for someone who is more or less self-employed: both rural and urban. I love the pioneer attitude here where everything just happens. This is where A. J. Hackett opened the first commercial bungy jump operation,[68] and all newspapers are locally owned. I live in the hills just outside Queenstown. And it is handy to be close to rural locations where you can go mountain biking and skiing, as well as stroll into town for a cappuccino in a pedestrian mall.

CHAPTER TWENTY-SEVEN

Dunedin and the Dalai Lama

A LL of these observations put me in mind of the fact that British or European culture, though the dominant influence, has not been the only influence on our cities. Auckland is described as the city with the largest Polynesian population (including Māori) and the largest city in Polynesia, as it is considerably larger than Honolulu. And there has also been an Asian influence on our cities as well as a British or European one. Again, Auckland these days is very multicultural in the sense of the size of its Asian as well as Polynesian populations. There is an authentic Chinese walled garden in Dunedin – the Dunedin Chinese Garden – which was opened in 2008. This is one of only three such gardens outside China, the other two being in Portland, Oregon and Vancouver, British Columbia.

I was also blessed by the Dalai Lama in Dunedin. The drive from Dunedin from Queenstown is beautiful, along Lake Waihola (a name that looks Hawai'ian but comes from a southern dialect of Māori) and what a sunrise it was that winter's day as I headed to the city early to catch the Dalai Lama's visit. I celebrate all religions and believe they are equally as important to acknowledge as cultural traditions. That is, I believe all religions should unite to save the world. I am happy to pray in any religious house.

I thought that about five hundred people would be at the church. Instead, when I got there, there were thousands of people. Many people could not hear the Dalai Lama speaking in the hall where he spoke afterward. I was

The Holy Dalai Lama in Dunedin

Ecumenical gathering with the Dalai Lama, Dunedin

Lake Waihola

told to put on a white scarf and then I got blessed, along with the multitude of course.

In the 1960s religion was still taken very seriously down south, though its influence has since waned. Both Christchurch and Dunedin began their existence as religious utopias of Anglicans and Presbyterians respectively, somewhat in the spirit of Salt Lake City, Utah. As in Boston, the founders of Christchurch were known as the 'Canterbury pilgrims', and fifty years ago, the Student Christian Movement was still the largest organisation on the Otago University campus in Dunedin.

In 1967 the Principal of Knox College Theological Hall in Dunedin, Lloyd Geering, faced what has been describes as the last trial for heresy in the Western world: that is to say, for 'doctrinal error and disturbing the peace of the church', proceedings held before the Doctrine Committee and the General Assembly of the Presbyterian Church in New Zealand, in Christchurch. Geering's trial was held in St Paul's Presbyterian Church, a Category 1 historic building erected in 1877 and demolished after the 2011 Christchurch earthquake. Geering was duly acquitted, you will be pleased to know.

Driving home along the beautiful roads, I was feeling blessed by more than just the Dalai Lama, and was already planning my next adventure.

CHAPTER TWENTY-EIGHT

Kaikoura Chaos and Christchurch Catastrophe

WITH all this talk of an urban culture and traditions, what of the earthquakes that have lately visited the South Island of New Zealand, the part of the country where the idea of towns and traditions runs most strongly?

Back in his day, Pevsner went on to describe the Cathedral of the Blessed Sacrament, Christchurch's Roman Catholic counterpart to the Anglican Cathedral, was described by Pevsner as "so large that I know of only one or two Roman Catholic churches in the whole of England that could compare with it. Its exterior is unquestionably provincial and awkward, but its interior with its two storeys of columns cannot be denied remarkable grandeur."

Well unfortunately the partly fallen remains of the Cathedral of the Blessed Sacrament feature prominently in Gerard Smyth's 2011 documentary about the Christchurch earthquakes, *When a City Falls*.

There were always portents of a looming disaster. New Zealand is, after all, prone to earthquakes. The Australians have long referred to New Zealand as 'the shaky isles'. No doubt this was done in an attempt to draw attention away from snakes, crocodiles and seven-year droughts, but there is more than a kernel of truth behind the famous Australian slur.

In 1888, almost as soon as it was built, the top was knocked off the Christchurch Anglican Cathedral spire by an earthquake.

In fact, the whole idea of constructing the cathedral in stone was quite controversial even at the time, as people thought that a wooden structure

A Portent of Things to Come. A view of Cathedral Square, looking southward, just after the earthquake of 1 September 1888. The top has been knocked off the top of the Anglican Cathedral's spire. Note also how well-established Christchurch's Cathedral Square already was by 1888, in essentially its present form. The building with double windows peeping past the cathedral tower survived until 1990, and the Post Office at right still survives. Source: Burton Brothers Studio, Dunedin. Te Papa registration number C.011676.)

would be more flexible and able to roll with the punches, as it were: a consideration that helps to explain why most colonial structures in the even more earthquake-prone North Island were made of wood.

The South Island colonists seem to have felt that no society erected entirely out of wood could ever be considered to be completely civilised and were prepared to take the risk of earthquakes.

And so, stone heritage of nineteenth-century origin is to be seen all over the South Island and not just in the relatively bigger and more prosperous cities such as Christchurch, Dunedin or Invercargill. Some of the best can be seen in smaller towns such as Oamaru, and even in isolated villages and country churches.

The North Islanders, themselves, forgot early reservations and started to build in brick, as did the South Islanders, until the 1931 Napier Earthquake put paid to the practice of building in brick in both islands by demonstrating the remarkable fragility of brick buildings with their thin, tall, slender walls.

In the television era, a stream of documentaries would stimulate awareness of earthquake hazard. In one 1977 documentary, the scientist Mr George Ivy explained that "under the North Island, we have the Pacific Plate going underneath the Indian Plate, and down in the far south-west of the South Island the two are the other way up, and we have the Indian Plate being forced under the Pacific Plate. The transition from one or [to] the other can only be described as rather a mess." In a 1980 television documentary, the head of civil defence in New Zealand, Major-General Robin Holloway, states that "I sometimes feel like that man who parades around the streets of London wearing a sandwich board saying 'Prepare to meet thy doom: the end of the world is nigh', and I sometimes feel that people take as much notice of me as they do of him. But somebody needs to be the conscience, because this danger of major disaster, from earthquakes and other causes, is very real."

Both of these older interviews were reprised in a prescient 1984 production which posited an earthquake disrupting road and rail transport through Kaikoura north of Christchurch for several weeks as has happened in the major earthquake of 2016.[69] The 1984 documentary used an image of disrupted tunnels at Kaikoura and a broken spire on the Christchurch Anglican Cathedral to symbolise the effects of the quake on the nearest big city: a valid enough point, even if this 1888-like image, which also put one in mind of the 1960s BBC clerical comedy *All Gas and Gaiters*, predicted something considerably milder than what really happened to Christchurch

The Sevicke-Jones building in Cathedral Square, an older brick building and one of a small number of buildings that collapsed more or less completely on 22 February 2011. Source: Lee Hanner via Wikimedia Commons CC-BY-SA 2.0, https://commons.wikimedia. org/wiki/ File:Christchurch_Earthquake_Sevicke_Jones_Building1.jpg

in 2011. A 1996 documentary also focused on Christchurch earthquake risks.[70]

To some extent these repeated warnings were successful. Older stone heritage buildings, often in government ownership by this stage, were generally strengthened to withstand earthquakes. Moreover, the construction of Victorian stone buildings was usually quite massive in any case. Their thick walls might well crack. But as long as they remained more or less upright, admittedly a big if in some cases, the crack could generally be filled in. And strict regulations were also applied to new buildings.

On the other hand, action to shore up pre-1931 brick buildings – the sorts of buildings typically owned or rented by small and struggling businesses with no money to spare for major reinforcement – was less forthcoming. For eighty years after 1931 *these* sorts of buildings had been sitting ducks for the next big earthquake to hit a city in New Zealand. How much longer would they sit?

Though many of the stone buildings were cracked and there were a few spectacular collapses, the greatest loss of life in the Christchurch earthquakes of 22 February 2011 was not associated with stone buildings, which had indeed often received significant anti-earthquake retrofitting in the past due to their heritage significance and were in any case for the most part fairly solid. It was to some extent associated with brick buildings of circa-1910 vintage: which are just as brittle as stone buildings but flimsier and less likely to have been retrofitted. But, most surprisingly, most of the loss of life occurred in a couple of modern multi-storey buildings that had completely failed to live up to their rated earthquake strength and 'pancaked'. Worst of all was the CTV Building on Madras Street, built in the mid-1980s, where all but one isolated stairwell crashed down to ground level. More than a

Cathedral Square, east side, shortly before the 2011 Earthquake.
(Avatar)

Cathedral Square after the 2011 Earthquake, looking eastward.

The tram in the preceding image was in the visible part of the street shown at the very top in this view, Worcester Street. (NZDF)

hundred died there, more than half the 185 fatalities that the earthquake caused on that fateful day.

It's tragic, in that regard, that something close to open season was declared on Christchurch heritage thereafter. As one of the aerial images above shows, much of central Christchurch has been bulldozed. Though 1980s buildings seemed to be the real killers, earthquake recovery minister Gerry Brownlee controversially argued that the most appropriate response to the 2011 earthquake was to carry out the mass demolition of "old dungers" dating back to the colonial period, sparing only a few heritage buildings of particular significance, which now stand mostly in isolation, like the last remnants of a forest.[71]

The scraped-bare look which downtown Christchurch soon acquired is mainly an artefact of emergency demolitions, not actual collapses. It has been widely and I think persuasively alleged that short-term penny pinching and an equally short-sighted desire to 'make progress', rather than public safety, lay behind a policy of wholesale heritage demolition under the aegis of emergency legislation.

In addition to brick buildings that were quite possibly beyond saving in many cases, and modern structures that had been compromised to the point of becoming economic write-offs, a considerable number of landmark stone heritage structures were demolished. These included Cranmer Court, a large L-shaped terrace of apartments and offices running part of the way along one side of Cranmer Square and down a neighbouring street. Formerly known as the Normal School – a school where student teachers sat in on the classes, a government school that set the norms of tuition – Cranmer Court was converted to apartments in the 1980s.[72]

As the Normal School, Cranmer Court had been built all the way back in the 1870s. It had already been earthquake-strengthened in the

*'185 Chairs': Peter Majendie's
unofficial memorial to people
killed on 22 February 2011*

*Reconstruction of a
clocktower on Madras
Street begins*

(Both images courtesy of Avatar)

course of conversion into apartments, and was listed as a Category One heritage building, the highest level of protection possible. The cost of its refurbishment after the 2011 earthquakes was estimated to be at most $5 million. Five million dollars is the equivalent of about a hundred metres of motorway, and not much for the revamp of a big building. But motorways were a higher priority for government than saving urban heritage. And so, Cranmer Court wound up on Brownlee's list of old dungers to be demolished. Cranmer Court and its demolition feature prominently in 'Heritage Matters', a 2013 episode of Paua Productions' series on the Christchurch earthquakes, *Aftermath*.

Failure to adequate defend Christchurch's heritage is a significant blot on the record of the recently-departed Prime Minister, John Key, who held that office for just over eight years from November 2008 until December 2016. Pundits praise Key for his seeming unflappability in the face of the Christchurch earthquakes. Episodes such as Cranmer Court betray the secret of this unflappability, namely, a *laissez-faire* approach in which the government did not work up much of a sweat about anything. It was up to the owners to save such a structure as Cranmer Court if they could find the ready money down at the bank. And if not, then not.

Would we roll up to a city in France, England or Germany and bowl the old stuff for any other reason than the immediate exingencies of a catastrophic war? Would we bowl the terraces of Bath, or the New Town of Edinburgh, because cracks were discovered? Would we fail to rebuild, say, Dresden, in the original style?

Well, it's just the same with Christchurch. It is not even valid to say that what the architectural historian Alex Bremner has dubbed the 'Imperial Gothic' of Christchurch and other such colonial cities is a first-rate imitation of the heritage architecture of a respectable old European town.[73] It is in essence the same thing.[74]

Just as all cities are young in Gordon McLauchlan's sense – those of countries like Germany often rebuilt, a city like Paris full of nineteenth century heritage no older than in Christchurch or Dunedin – so we can equally say that in terms of an ongoing urban culture and its traditions and gardens, that pre-2011 Christchurch and an old European town did not look the same. They *were* the same.

Sadly, Christchurch is no longer the capital of New Zealand's nineteenth century to the extent that it once was. As the famous line from *Casablanca* goes, "we'll always have Paris:" but, as was meant in the film, we will have

Christchurch Re:START Mall in Cashel Street (2013).

Public domain image by 'Pear285' (https://commons.wikimedia. org/wiki/File:ReSTART_City_Mall_Christchurch_2013.jpg)

Effects of the 2016 earthquake in Kaikoura. A massive slip blocks the coastal road, and new land uplifted several metres from the sea appears as dark red, because it is covered in dead or dying seaweed.
(NZDF: image 20161114_NZDF_S1015650_016)

it in fond memory. Hopefully nothing so drastic will befall what was, prior to 2011, probably the second-most architecturally-significant nineteenth-century townscape in New Zealand, that of Dunedin.

On a more positive note, innovation springs eternal. A city like Christchurch does not entirely inhabit the past by any means. There has been an upsurge of innovation, and community togetherness, and rebellion against official insensitivity. On the modern side of things, one of the most interesting things to happen in Christchurch has been the innovative use of shipping containers to produce, quite early on, the Restart Container Mall in Cashel Street, which sprang up almost immediately after the great earthquake, in 2011. Like the steel drums of the West Indies, fashioned from oil drums in World War II, this is a new leg of cultural development in Christchurch, a city often mocked with some validity as being stuck in the past. A new, innovative modernism has now taken hold in a city that used to have a rather staid reputation, so perhaps things will work out well in the long run.

CHAPTER TWENTY-NINE
Aoraki / Mount Cook
ANOTHER DEADLY PEAK

Mount Cook Region. Map data ©2016 Google. Localities added.

I WENT to Mt Cook in January 2013 to do a five-day New Zealand Alpine Club High Alpine Skills training course, primarily because I was trying to prepare myself to climb Mont Blanc in France. In addition to Mont Blanc, I wanted to climb Mount Aspiring in New Zealand, which I did also attempt, though it turned out to be an absolute disaster because of hired crampons that broke, of which more below.

I had only done a basic Stage 1 and Stage 2 course previously. Because I hadn't completed a Stage 3 course where I would have stayed outside in a snow cave, I didn't have any of that experience and just jumped straight from Stage 2 to the High Alpine Skills (Stage 3 is in between).

Anyway, the High Alpine Skills course was horrendous because of the additional experience which I should have been made to acquire first, in hindsight. There were about eight of us on the course and there were two others who were in the same boat as me, having not done the Stage 3 course either. One guy from Wellington was just as lost as I was. I had rock-climbing boots but I'd never even done a rock-climbing wall before, and all of a sudden I had crampons on and was expected to go up rocks.

We learnt knots, but I really didn't like them and just got stressed out and forgot them. I didn't have any confidence whatsoever and the knots were seriously confusing. I struggled especially when they tried teaching us how to prusik up a rope – a technique of climbing a rope using looped hitches which you'd need if you fell down a crevice – I was completely lost!

We started our High Alpine Skills training course near Mt Cook Village, staying at the New Zealand Alpine Club's hut called Unwin Lodge, which was a very eerie place. Every time I had stayed there, I couldn't believe the people I met that had seen such dreadful accidents happen. I was sitting in the lounge and a party of four climbers came up and were let in sombrely by the hut warden, as they had lost someone on the mountain. It was the sort of place where death was quite a frequent occurrence.

Before the course started, I remember talking to a woman about the fact that there was no women's alpine training course. Then we started talking about boots because I started with a pair that didn't fit me. I couldn't find a proper fit anywhere, due to bunions. I still haven't got a pair which fit me, which has been a major problem for my climbing. I told the woman that I was going to get blisters that would be beyond repair before I even got up the mountain, but she said that was just part and parcel of it. She was in her fifties and told me the next issue would be finding a climbing partner, which was something she'd found very difficult. She said she climbed with people who were around 25 years old and were generally a lot more fit than her.

I won't forget what she told me about a climb she had done with a partner. As with diving, you always climb with a partner too (at the very least, somebody has to hold the other end of the rope!) She said they had pitched their tent half under a flat rock face and half out in the open and an avalanche had come down and completely covered her climbing partner. She had to dig her out and said they were lucky to be alive because they both could have died. I remember thinking, 'Oh, this climbing business is *quite* risky'; for generally I am fairly conservative when it comes to taking risks.

As New Zealand's tallest mountain, Mt Cook/Aoraki has long offered a challenge for aspiring climbers. To Ngāi Tahu, the peak represents the most sacred of ancestors and it is therefore tapu (forbidden) to climb on its head. Government cultural guidelines recommend not standing right at the top, not cooking or eating right at the top, and to take out all rubbish (which people should do anyway). All the same, European explorers have come to the area from the time of earliest settlement until now to attempt the climb. These include Sir Edmund Hillary, who learnt his mountain-craft on Mt Cook and its surrounding peaks. The Aoraki/Mt Cook National Park itself was established in 1953 to protect the mountainous area, even though some of the land in the park is still privately owned.

To start with, we trekked some way up the nearby Sealy Range, and my feet became covered in blisters. We did some training and learnt belaying, and then tramped back down to Unwin Lodge. From Unwin Lodge, flew by helicopter up and over the charming Sealy Tarns to the Barron Saddle Hut to start our alpine training in earnest.

Once we got there, we found out that an earlier hut at a nearby location, the Three Johns Hut, had been blown over a precipice by the wind in 1977. Three people inside at the time were killed. Huts on Mt Cook have also been taken out by avalanches.

The Barron Saddle Hut, a sort of metal cylinder which looked like it was built to handle extreme natural forces, had lately had some of its windows blown in, or sucked out, and they were covered over by wood. I got no sleep whatsoever at first, worrying about all this.

From the hut, we went via Barron Saddle to stay overnight on Mt Annette on the Sealy Range. There was a beautiful sunset over the Mt Cook/Aoraki mountain range, I had taken what was known as a bivvy with me, which is

Tramping back to the Unwin Lodge

The High Alpine Skills course class photo

Learning knots

One of the Sealy Tarns

*The Barron
Saddle Hut*

*A closer view of the
Barron Saddle Hut
with its damaged
windows*

*Sleeping out under
the stars*

a sleeping bag which zips over, but had I left it behind in Barron Saddle Hut because I was so tired. In the end, I had to borrow an emergency blanket off one of the instructors, Jim Mason, who also runs an HR company and works for the army. I just wrapped it around me and our group slept outside under the stars that night, huddled together. It was beautiful, though cold. But I had enough clothes on, about three or four layers, to cope. The instructors were more than professional, keeping an extra eye on people like me who were relatively inexperienced. After getting nervous initially due to the unnerving Unwin Lodge incident and the history of Barron Saddle, I felt completely safe in the hands of the instructors.

It had been quite an adventure and Mt Cook was stunning, but the whole time I just didn't feel comfortable with my level of alpine skills. I haven't given up on that sort of thing, but I'm going to take a step back and think I'm better off with a guide in such mountainous areas. I'll probably need to get some better climbing boots too because at the end of the alpine course it took my feet a month to repair from all the blisters I had from my shoes.

Having done all this, I am in awe of early climbers who ascended these mountains in hobnailed boots (crampons weren't invented till later). Progressively more elaborate arrangements of nails gradually evolved into the removable crampons we are familiar with today.

Climbers also ascended in long skirts and generally respectable looking attire if they were women in the Victorian era, as surprisingly many were. A more informal look had come in by the 1930s, however.

Speaking of crampons, this reminds me of the disastrous episode I had with some hired crampons in 2013 which both came apart when I was ascending Mount Aspiring with an Alpine guide named Murray Ball, an incident which received some coverage in the media.[75]

'Mountaineering Group' photographed by Joseph James Kinsey, circa 1895, unidentified New Zealand location. From left, rear, Matthias Zurbriggen, unidentified, Jack Clarke. From left, front, 'Signor Borsalino', unidentified, May Kinsey, unidentified. Zurbriggen and Clarke are names in New Zealand alpinism; Clarke was part of the first party to summit Mount Cook in 1894 and Zurbriggen, a Swiss, was among other things the first to summit Mt Aconcagua, the highest peak in South America. J. J. Kinsey was a Christchurch businessman deeply involved in the organisation of the Antarctic expeditions of Scott and Shackleton, later knighted for services to polar exploration. (Reference PA1-q-137-66-1, Alexander Turnbull Library, http://mp.natlib.govt.nz/detail/?id=30822).

Though I had paid a lot of money to be guided up Aspiring, the window of opportunity to climb the mountain closed in the time it took for my guide to achieve a field repair of the crampons. I laid a complaint with the Small Claims Tribunal but only received back the crampon hire fee,

Freda du Faur, the first woman to climb Aoraki / Mount Cook.

Photograph by George Mannering circa 1910, Canterbury Museum, Christchurch, NZ

which was a pittance, and not compensation for money effectively wasted on Murray's fee (which was very much greater) since I was not now able to get to the top, and a holiday spoiled.

There were some quite interesting technical questions that unfortunately never got a proper airing in the small claims tribunal, probably because they were too technical. Having crampons come apart is a known issue in the mountaineering community. It is one of those things that *can* happen since crampons come in two parts with an adjustment bar in between, held by a spring clip with a peg that passes through one of a series of holes in the bar.

So, from time to time they *will* come apart if the crampons are worn, not properly adjusted, take a beating, and so forth. The spring clip can become tired, and the housing that houses the spring mechanism can also become worn. Excessive build-up of snow can also push the peg out of the hole, which is why climbers routinely tap their crampons with their ice axe

305

to shake snow loose; and there are also plates and rubber accordion-type covers to help keep snow out of the works.

Murray said that the crampons I had hired had indeed suffered from a form of wear that was normally undetectable; while the person I hired them off claimed that they were fine and that they had popped apart due

'Mount Oates Mountaineering Party at the Mingha River', 15 February 1931. From left, Betsy Blunden, John Dobree Pascoe and an unidentified individual. Betsy Blunden was the first woman to work as a guide at Mount Cook, from 1928 onward, and the world's first female alpine guide. Pascoe would go on to become a famous photographer. (Reference PA1-o-407-089-5, Alexander Turnbull Library)

The beginning of my planned Mount Aspiring climb

Kea at Colin Todd Hut

Looking towards Mounts Barff and Liverpool

Murray doing his best to fix my failed crampons

The summit of Mount Aspiring – we were so close!

The crampons which I still believe were defective and could have killed me

to misuse. Nobody really knew for a fact what had happened: but by the same token nobody really seemed all that keen to spend much time on the issue, and nobody wanted to refund my guide's fees either.

It would have cost as much as the cost of the hire fees at issue to call in a consulting engineer or any other kind of expert witness, which it seems to me is what would have been needed to really find out what had happened and who was at fault. In the absence of science, the whole business became quite personally unpleasant instead.

To my mind this whole incident says quite a lot about the inadequately organised and inadequately guaranteed nature of adventure tourism in New Zealand. Though there are many fine people out there, basically if something goes wrong, the tourist often doesn't have much comeback.

What does it take to get redress and accountability beyond the almost token level of the refund of crampon hire fees? Why is there not some system of official engineering inspection that kicks in, in a case like this: or at the very least, a guarantee scheme that refunds *all* the money lost, and not just the price of the straw that broke the camel's back?

I eventually won the case but only to the point of having the princely sum of my crampon hire refunded. The technical issues concerning the crampons were never clarified in the Disputes Tribunal, which is not competent to get into that level of engineering detail.

Unfortunately, there is nothing in current New Zealand legislation that ensures a proper guarantee for tourists and clients in this sort of situation. Were the crampons really a bit past it? Nobody knows.

New Zealand's tourism industry is very much pitched toward adventurous, risky and once-in-a-lifetime experiences. Yet, as with an under-funded DOC whose bridges tip over, it seems that everything is a bit stretched thin and run too much in a spirit of buyer beware, attitudes possibly inherited from the buccaneering days of the past and compounded by the wider political fashion for deregulation since the 1980s.

I'm far from being the only person to say this. You read it all the time in newspaper editorials, letters and articles.

For instance, why isn't there a competent engineering inspectorate that vets things like hired crampons and thus removes all doubt, or that has a mandate to perform proper engineering inspections if they break? I'm thinking of something along the lines of marine certification or warrants of fitness for cars, except that what I am proposing would be for equipment used in the outdoors and the wilderness: hired equipment in particular. In other words, there's plenty of precedent.

Why is it not possible to offer a refund on the cost of a whole trip if an equipment failure ruins somebody's holiday? That is to say, if that equipment failure is indeed the thing that goes wrong, to the point of spoiling the whole trip.

A government agency charged with upholding the good name of 'New Zealand Inc' should be able to offer such a guarantee – especially if the gear has got the tick from an official inspection agency beforehand.

In many European countries, there is a government-run travel guarantee fund that guarantees package tours. However, New Zealand is not really package tour country. We attract many independent travellers, and there is a need to think about the reputation of 'New Zealand Inc'. *New Zealand* is the package.

A more organised system of checks and guarantees seems especially relevant to the New Zealand hire trade. Everyone in the outdoors seems to agree that with the best will in the world there is always more of a risk of failure with hired gear from any shop, simply because nobody really knows how it has been treated. And the customer usually can't tell how old it is either.

It's always better to have your own and look after it (and not leave it behind!). But there will always be a hire trade. So, there should be a more robust system of government guarantees, both while gear is in service and after something breaks as well.

MARY JANE WALKER

CHAPTER THIRTY
Matukituki Valley

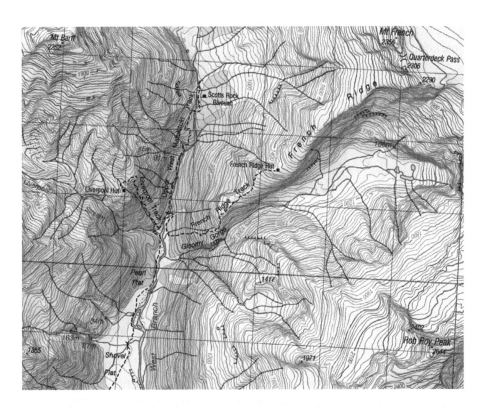

Liverpool Track, West Matukituki Track and French Ridge Track.
Also shown are Mount Barff (top left), Mount French (top right) and
Rob Roy Peak (bottom right). (LINZ via NZTopomaps.com, March 2017)

M Y first tramp into Mount Aspiring National Park was with the Upper Clutha Tramping Club, a group of older farmers based out of Wanaka. All of them were between 70 and 85 years old, so I was easily the youngest of the group! They were good people though – I think farmers are friendlier than the professionals I've met in other tramping clubs. They also seemed to co-exist better than another club I had recently left, whose members spent more time complaining than tramping!

We began our tramp into the Matukituki Valley near Mt Aspiring from the Raspberry Creek Carpark, which is an hour's drive from Wanaka. It was an incredible drive, too, up a half-unsealed road with Rob Roy Peak and Mt Aspiring on the right, and another set of mountain ranges to the left. Once we parked our cars and entered the valley, we made our way towards Aspiring Hut, which used to be managed by the New Zealand Alpine Club along with the French Ridge Hut (which is just below the Bonar Glacier on the approach to Mt Aspiring). The other hut in the valley is Liverpool Hut, tucked in below Mt Liverpool, and they are now all under DOC management.

The Matukituki Valley is an ancient place, first used by early Māori as a hunting ground for native birds such as tūī and kākāpō. These Māori were the first to name Mt Aspiring, calling it Tititea, which means 'steep peak of glistening white'. The valley was later settled by Europeans for farming, and its natural features were recognised nationally in 1964 when the Mt Aspiring National Park was created.

From the Raspberry Creek carpark, we tramped up the valley through grassland flats and across small bluffs to Aspiring Hut, a short nine-kilometre hike of about two hours. To get to the other huts in the valley, you need to hike to Pearl Flat, which is another short hike of five kilometres and then the track forks off towards Liverpool Hut, French Ridge and the head of the Matukituki Valley.

Another striking feature of this area is Sharks Tooth Peak, which rises to 2,096m and is particularly impressive from the Raspberry carpark. It's located to the east of the Main Divide.

However, for my first tramp into the valley with the Upper Clutha Tramping Club, we went up towards the Cascade Saddle from Aspiring Hut. The track forks off in two directions, with one leading deeper up the valley towards Pearl Flat and the other huts, and the other towards the Cascade Saddle, which links the Matukituki with the Rees-Dart Tracks. This route climbs above Mount Aspiring Hut and over a high alpine pass into the Dart Valley, stopping at the Dart Hut on the Rees-Dart. It's a long hike, too, people should expect it to take about ten to twelve hours to complete. Despite this, many people trek without a pack and only sometimes remember to bring water. I've met many backpackers walking in sandshoes and without the appropriate gear coming over the Cascade Saddle – it amazes me how unprepared some people are!

On one occasion about a year ago, when I camped out near the Dart Hut on the Dart Glacier, I met a paid DOC warden sitting beside the track. He told me that a volunteer warden was flying in to relieve him, which I found astonishing as I'd previously tried to become a relief hut warden on this track. As such I was pretty fired up by the time I got to the Dart Hut.

Despite not being able to volunteer in the Matukituki Valley or on the nearby Rees-Dart Track, I fully enjoyed my first tramp into the area with the Upper Clutha Tramping Club. The walk from the Raspberry carpark to the Cascade Saddle was beautiful, and I took some very nice photos of the natural features near the track.

My second tramp into the Matukituki Valley was in July 2013, and I was tramping solo as I'd wanted to explore the area but didn't have anyone to go with. However, I actually found that it made the tramp much easier because some of those huts can get quite full – especially the Aspiring Hut because it's only two hours from the carpark.

In the Matukituki Valley

In the Matukituki Valley (my father Brian below)

I tramped to Aspiring Hut and stayed there where I got to know Stu, the volunteer DOC warden for the hut. There was a thriving bird population near the hut because he kills the wild cats – mostly by shooting them rather than setting traps, too. He showed me one he'd just shot and I really could

Up the Matukituki Valley – the Rob Roy Glacier is visible in the view above

*Up the
Matukituki Valley,
with another fine
view of Rob Roy*

see why trapping them wouldn't work, it just wouldn't kill these pests who are a danger to the native wildlife. This made me want to get my own gun licence for the next time I volunteer as a hut warden – something I'd like to do after I've finished this book.

This time, instead of taking the Saddle, I carried on from Aspiring Hut to the new Liverpool Hut, which was an incredible walk despite being quite steep and slippery in parts. It is a beautiful place with incredible views, and I got a good shot of Mt Aspiring and Mt Liverpool on my camera. I took plenty of photos of Liverpool Hut and its surroundings, one of which I later submitted to the New Zealand Alpine Club's website and it became the inspiration for them to hold competitions on hut photography.

After I finished there, I wasn't quite ready to end my tramp. I decided instead I would climb Mt French, and then headed down the valley to find the French Ridge Track.

CHAPTER THIRTY-ONE
French Ridge

Photo showing French Ridge Hut, under my ice axe

MY tramp up to French Ridge Hut was quite difficult, as the track was coated with spiny plants native to New Zealand called speargrass, which gets very slippery underfoot when it snows. The track was also filled with mountaineers who, like me, wanted to climb Mount French. I had brought my ice axe along, and wanted to practice my skills with it on the mountain.

The French Ridge Track forks off to the right from Pearl Flat in the Matukituki Valley, and was around a 3.2-kilometre walk from the Liverpool Hut where I'd come from. From the flat, trampers ford the Liverpool stream or cross over on a swing bridge to the track, and climb for a few hours through bush and subalpine terrain to reach the French Ridge Hut. The hut offers spectacular views of the nearby Mount French, ironically named after John French, a British army officer who was afraid of heights and never stepped foot on the mountain.[76] The climb is only a five to six-hour return trip from French Ridge Hut, heading up towards Quarterdeck Pass and then along a snowy ridge to the summit. Although not a prominent peak itself, Mount French is an incredible viewing platform for the nearby Mount Aspiring and Bonar Glacier, and is often climbed by mountaineers in consolation for not making it to these.

I met two such climbers from Australia at French Ridge Hut, who had attempted to climb Mount Aspiring using just their rock climbing skills. They got stuck halfway up the mountain on a rock without any rope, and had to be helped down by a nearby Norwegian guide who was taking a New Zealand woman up the mountain. He stopped his ascent to throw them a line, and once they were off the rock, they slid down on the snow and were just gliding over crevasses in their haste to descend the mountain! The guide and the New Zealand woman just couldn't believe that people would descend in such a foolhardy manner, and were amazed they didn't fall down any of the crevasses!

While I was at the hut, I met a mother of two who also used to rock-climb and had attempted to climb Mount Aspiring. She didn't make the summit either because it was too windy. However, she said she'd done it just for the experience and that she climbed for the journey, not the peak – something I thought was a great principle to have!

I really was amongst interesting company at French Ridge Hut. As well as the rock climbers, there was a man who lived in the woods in Norway, and a policeman from Auckland who had come down with three friends to climb Mt Aspiring. However, he had decided not to climb because he hadn't been out on a mountain for over 10 years. It was quite a wise decision to make, really, especially as he had a young family to take care of and his wife hadn't wanted him to go.

While his friends headed towards Mount Aspiring, the policeman climbed up Mount French on the side of the Bonar Glacier, which could have easily caused an avalanche. A woman coming down with a guide had seen this and gave him a right talking to for endangering all of us by taking this reckless path instead of using the existing steps. I certainly followed the stairs when I climbed Mount French, as climbing in the snow is easier if you just follow the track!

Later, two mountaineers with thirty kilogramme packs came into the hut, and I don't think I've ever eaten as much as I did that evening! They offered me a pistachio nut spread and all sorts of other food and, seeing as I usually hike with only just enough food for the tramp, it was like a feast! I decided to stay there for a couple of days after that.

Another mountaineer I met was a man named Dean who had been up Mt Everest about eight or nine times, and was on the French Ridge Track as a guide. He was with a guy from Australia who had done three weeks of mountaineering and was trying to get to the top of Mt Aspiring. I talked to Dean for a bit, and his stories made me think I really would not want to be a guide. Imagine being stuck with some awkward character for weeks and be paid to keep them company and psyche them to the top – it would just drive me batty!

I left French Ridge Hut having thoroughly enjoyed my time in the mountains, thinking about how I'd love to climb Mount Aspiring one day. I made good time on the way down, but was still deep into the Matukituki Valley when night fell, and then all of a sudden, my torch went out. I had brought two with me but the first had died days earlier, so I was left scrambling down the valley in the dark. To make things worse, it also started raining. I resigned myself to the fact that I'd probably have to sleep out in the rain, not having brought a tent. However, I did have an emergency blanket which you can buy for just ten dollars. I felt pretty good about using this if I had to, and was preparing to sleep outside in the rain under a tree. However, I thankfully made it back to my car and didn't have to spend a wet night in the valley after all.

CHAPTER THIRTY-TWO
Gillespie Pass and Wilkin Valley
HARD YAKKA, BUT STILL THE BEST ALPINE FLOWERS

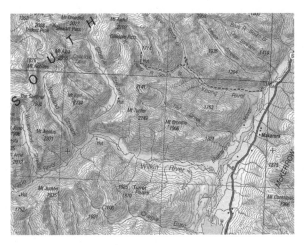

*The Siberia, Wilkin and Young Valleys with Gillespie Pass
and Crucible Lake / Lake Crucible, Lake Wanaka at bottom.*
(LINZ via NZTopomaps.com, March 2017)

*Intersection of the Wilkin River and Siberia Stream, South
Island, looking northward.* Google Earth Screenshot in 3D view.
Imagery ©2017 DigitalGlobe. Map data ©2017 Google

I DON'T usually begin my tramping with a helicopter ride, but then again, my one-week stint as a volunteer DOC warden at Siberia Hut was an adventure of a different kind. I was in the attractive Wilkin and Young Valleys in the Mt Aspiring National Park, which contained both the hut I was to be working in and the magnificent Gillespie Pass Circuit. Located near Makarora at the head of Lake Wanaka, this 58-kilometre circuit takes three to four days to complete, and retraces the steps of ancient Māori from Otago and Southland who used to visit the area to hunt and fish. While I didn't complete the whole track, I was planning to do the Gillespie Pass as part of my role as a DOC hut warden and so I had a key to the Young Hut also.

While in the valley I met a lot of people who were working for DOC, many of them in the Makarora Office, which used to employ 10 people. There was a ranger called Chris who had lived with his wife in the Makarora community for a number of years, as had most of his co-workers, an exception being an English girl working there as a warden named Coreen with whom I became good friends. From Makarora, I flew into Siberia Hut by helicopter and took a great photo of the beautiful Crucible Lake, or Lake Crucible – both names are used interchangeably, even in official maps and guides – which was dotted with ice. Behind it you could see Mt Dreadful, which is 2,020 metres high and to the left of Mount Crucible, and then to the right of Young Hut, which we also passed over, you could see Mount Awful. From the helicopter the full mountain range was a magnificent sight, though I wasn't too keen on the names!

I was dropped off near Siberia Hut by the helicopter and given a locator beacon. I was also informed beforehand that there were also some men there doing some DOC work for the week. They were to do some building, take out rubbish and helicopter in picnic tables. I thought to myself, 'Hang on.

The Wilkin River from the helicopter (above); Spot the deer (below)

Gillespie(above); Lake Crucible (below)

I've made a sacrifice being a volunteer and I don't feel that I should have to share my hut with three other people.' Anyway, the guys ended up sleeping in the main hut as it wasn't overcrowded.

As I generally do when working as a DOC warden, I had asked to be given some possum traps. 'Oh, there's no possums here,' Chris had said. I had thought, 'Surely there must be!' I had met a guy named Tussock on my way out of the Rees-Dart Track who had told me about how DOC hadn't done any poison-baiting in the Eglinton Valley further south and they almost lost the mōhua (yellowhead), which is a rare native bird. Tussock lived in Glenorchy and had worked for DOC part-time in the valley, which is part of the Lower Hollyford Track, for thirty years.

Close-up of Lake Crucible – note the floating ice

As part of his work in the Eglinton Valley and on the Routeburn Track also, Tussock had to put out plastic tunnels which measure the number of rats or mice that come through a particular area as the animals run through them. He told me that some of the native trees periodically produces more seeds than usual, a phenomenon known as 'mast', and that in former times this provided an ample food supply which encouraged the native birds to breed in that year. Nowadays, however, the mast phenomenon mainly produces an oversupply of rats and mice. This then brings more ferrets and stoats which eat the rodents. However, once the rats and mice have all been eaten, the predators turn to the native birds which not only miss out on some of the mast but then have the eggs and chicks that they do manage to produce eaten as well. So, if the predators aren't controlled by trapping, it's easy to see why the mōhua in Eglinton became endangered. The kākā, forest-dwelling relatives of the kea, were in trouble as well.

That was a very interesting conversation. And Tussock had also told me that there were rock wrens at the top of Gillespie Pass in the Wilkin/Young area. The Gillespie Pass goes over from Siberia Hut to Young Hut and takes about six to eight hours to tramp, climbing up twelve kilometres through forest up to the 1,600 metres-high ridge before descending into the upper Young Valley where the hut is. I remember on the first day tramping to Lake Crucible, which is three to four hours away from Siberia Hut through the beautiful Siberia Valley, being completely blown away by seeing ice in an alpine lake. However, it was the Gillespie Pass that most astounded me. It was the most beautiful pass that I'd ever been on in the country, and the blooms and the mountain lilies up there were just fantastic. That was a beautiful day's walk; for I did not carry on but went back to Siberia Hut. There weren't so many visitors at that time of the year, but this hut does get overcrowded in the summer.

After that, I trekked over to Kerin Forks Hut, which is a two to three hour walk of some seven kilometres from Siberia Hut, passing through a forest and above Siberia Gorge. This beautiful old hut sits only four hundred metres downstream from the Siberia Stream/Wilkin River junction, which has been identified as being notoriously difficult to cross and especially prone to flooding since at least as far back as 1967.[77] So, it was interesting going along the Wilkin River, which I had already seen from the air in my helicopter ride to Siberia Hut.

After returning to Siberia Hut, I went over the Gillespie Pass to Young Hut where I was a DOC warden for a few more days, and then I went back over the Gillespie Pass to Wilkin Hut. At Young Hut, DOC had employed a warden who told me she didn't kill possums. In spite of official insistence that there were no possums in the valley, I'd left out two live traps which had both caught possums (by live trap I mean the sort of trap that catches an animal and imprisons it in a box, unharmed). So, possums definitely were in the valley and I was very surprised that DOC had assumed there weren't any. I left the possums in the trap (alive) as proof, and told the warden about them on my way out.

There is also an argument going on in DOC whether you shouldn't employ officers who won't kill animals, as possums do endanger our birdlife and need to be controlled.

I signed out but was sad to leave the valley, as I'd made good friends with Coreen. Most of the other wardens had become good friends with her also, so it was really sad when she lost her job only six months later, despite having a degree in parks and recreation. The morale going through DOC even now is very low and I feel extremely sorry for wardens because they have so many jobs to do with the increase of tourists coming to our country. New Zealand wants another million tourists to come in, increasing overseas tourist numbers by half as much again over current levels.[78] In 2016, the government cut the DOC budget by another $34 million.[79] However, there was a change of government in 2017 in favour of a three-party coalition, and the memorandum of understanding between the Labour and Green parties, a key part of the coalition framework, contains the phrase "Budget provision will be made for significantly increasing the Department of Conservation's funding."[80]

CHAPTER THIRTY-THREE

Rees-Dart

THE MOST BEAUTIFUL GLACIER

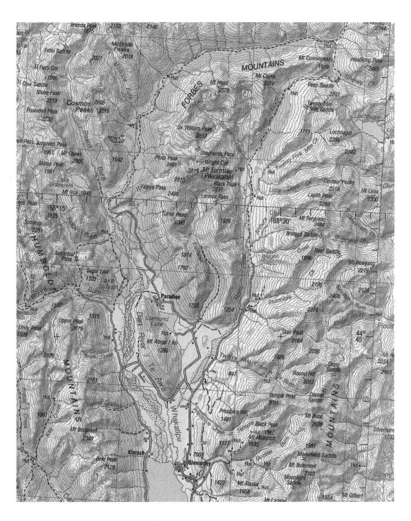

The Valleys of the Rees and the Dart surround the Forbes Mountains, north of Glenorchy and Lake Wakatipu. (LINZ via NZTopomaps.com, Feb. 2017)

333

I WAS cold and boggy underfoot as I and a few tramping friends began our tramp on the great Rees-Dart Track near Glenorchy. It was a gloomy beginning to the walk trudging through the mud alongside the aptly-named Muddy Creek, so we were all relieved when we reached the welcoming Shelter Rock Hut. A good fire was blazing in the lounge, and after dinner I fell asleep quickly in the warm hut, worn out from our seven-hour hike.

Some people came into the hut at two o'clock in the morning, but they were so considerate to us and were very quiet. I couldn't believe it when I met them the next morning and found out it was a group of eight! They said they had left at four o'clock in the afternoon, and were walking with torches for most of the way. Well, that was no easy walk, and I certainly wouldn't have wanted to have been tramping it at midnight, especially on a night without a full moon!

The route which this group had tramped in the dark runs from Muddy Creek through marshy flatland and joins with the Rees River at the Mount Aspiring National Park boundary. From there it's another seven kilometres hiking to Shelter Rock, the first hut on the four-day Rees-Dart Track. Part of the South Island's World Heritage area, the Rees and Dart Valleys were first used by the Ngāi Tahu people of Murihiku/Southland and Otago for hunting moa and collecting greenstone.[81] Alongside its English name, the Dart River has an official Māori name which also appears on maps, Te Awa Whakatipu, meaning the W[h]akatipu River or the river that drains into Lake Wakatipu.

The now-you-see-it, now-you-don't presence of the letter 'h' in W[h]akatipu points to a certain obscurity in the meaning of the lake's name, which on the face of it means waka-tipu or expanding hollow, perhaps even 'growing canoe', but is thought more likely to be a southern dialect version of whanga-tipu meaning expanding bay, as heard and written down by some Otago pioneer. And so, the New Zealand Government's Geographic Board has ruled that the Māori spelling of the lake's chief tributary shall be the Awa Whakatipu, whaka- with an 'h' being the more officially-accepted southern version of whanga-.

(Whakatipu can also mean something like personal growth, being self-made or 'rising through the ranks', though in that case the initial particle whaka- has a different meaning. That is probably not the origin of Lake Wakatipu's name.)

All this suggests that, in theory, Lake Wakatipu should be renamed Lake Whakatipu to be consistent with the dominant theory of how it got its name. Māori place-names thought to be corrupt or incorrect are quite frequently amended by the Geographic Board: thus, the town of Koiterangi, notorious as the site of the 1940s massacre and manhunt portrayed in the 1981 film *Bad Blood*, long ago became Kowhitirangi. But these name changes have generally only affected obscure localities up to now: localities where, as in the case of Koiterangi, the locals might also in some cases have been quite happy to acquire a new address or at least not greatly affected by a name change in any day to day sense. In contrast, the recent renaming of the North Island city of Wanganui to Whanganui created an enormous controversy in view of the familiarity of the old name; and so, it might be that officialdom has decided to let sleeping dogs lie in the almost identical case of Lake Wakatipu/Whakatipu. Any name change for the lake, even a minor one, would surely not be popular with the tourism industry.

In any case the idea of something growing, expanding, opening out and becoming huge seems common to all theories of how Lake Wakatipu got its name, whether this name should have an 'h' in it or not. It is an idea that surely reflects the local glacial topography of big lakes and big valleys.

After the region around the lake was first colonised by Māori, European settlers would come looking for gold and farmland. One of these, Patrick Caples, was the first to make a written record of the magnificent Dart Glacier when crossing the valley with a mining party. From 1899 until 1902 a gold dredge operated on the Dart River, and its remains can still be seen today.

We left Shelter Rock at about eight o'clock the next morning to make our way to Dart Hut. Heading over the Rees Saddle we encountered a light dusting of snow on the track. Now, I have had experience tramping in snow and done some alpine training, but I hadn't brought any crampons with me on the Rees-Dart, which made the ascent quite risky all the same.

If it had kept snowing, things would have been a lot worse, but as it was this section of the tramp was hard enough. Adding to the danger was quite a steep drop-off at three different points along the Saddle. New Zealand doesn't have ropes to hold onto like Mt Blanc or other parts of Europe I've tramped – no, here the Rees-Dart is classed as a backcountry track! Thankfully, we managed to descend the Saddle safely and re-joined the track down to Dart Hut. It was quite a long day of tramping, but it certainly was a beautiful walk, with the snow only adding to the already spectacular mountain scenery.

I found a bunk in the Dart Hut, where we were to spend two nights, and decided to take a look at the Dart Glacier. The glacier is up towards the Cascade Saddle, which I'd often thought about going to, and is only a three hour walk from the hut. Along the way, I met a young Indonesian-born Chinese woman who I was in complete awe of – at only fifteen years old she had already tramped most of the Great Walks in the South Island! At the end of the day, I guess you just have to get out there and do it.

We finally reached the Dart Glacier and I fell absolutely in love with it. As we climbed up towards the Cascade Saddle, the glacier turned from rock and scree into an icy, white slash in the landscape. However, it wasn't until we reached the top of the Saddle that the alpine views were fully exposed, and it was an impressive sight! Looking out from the ridge, we could see one side of Mount Aspiring on our left, the Matukituki Valley on our right, and the incredible Dart Glacier below us. All in all, it was an incredible view – even from the precariously located Cascade Saddle Toilet! No wonder the Mount Aspiring National Park is one of my favourite places, with such incredible natural features.

We made it back to Dart Hut, and I carried on to Daley's Flat Hut, which felt like a different walk altogether. Between the two huts, and all the way through to Chinaman's Bluff, you follow a faint track through sprawling beech forests and across terraces – very different from the snow-covered Rees Saddle we had crossed earlier!

Although my time at Dart Hut had been uneventful, when I had previously tramped the Rees-Dart Track with the Upper Clutha Tramping Club, I had had an interesting encounter with the volunteer DOC warden there: a large, blonde woman. She had asked me how much the backcountry hut pass tickets were, so I told her the price. Then she promptly walked around at five p.m. and asked everyone in the hut if they'd signed in and paid their tickets! She didn't really know what she was doing, because that was generally done at 7.30 p.m. as a precaution to ensure that trampers who had left the Mount Aspiring Hut had made it – or at least so you'd have time to check in on them via radio.

Anyway, she didn't bother checking on anyone who came in late. One English tramper who had left the carpark only slightly later than us, reached the hut at 5.30pm and wondered why the warden didn't sign him in. I told him they don't tick you off in New Zealand. You have to be reported missing by somebody else with whom you have deposited your plans (which generally only happens if you don't make it back from the entire trip), and if you don't make it to the next hut and nobody knows you are missing, you can easily become just another fatality. That's why I always carry a locator beacon with me when out tramping and I told the Englishman he should do the same.

Half an hour later, an Israeli guy rushed into the hut wanting to call out the rescue helicopter because his friends were still out on the Rees Saddle. I told him to knock on the warden's door, but she just told him he'd have to wait. Finally, they turned up at around 9.00 pm, not even carrying a sleeping bag!

These under-prepared trampers really could have got in some serious trouble because, although it's a beautiful and varied walk, the Rees-Dart Track can be dangerous, just like any mountainous area. The track often floods, creating hazardous conditions for river crossers. The route over the Cascade Saddle has also claimed a number of lives. As such, DOC recommends that everyone venturing into the Rees-Dart area pay close attention to the weather and take extreme care when crossing rivers, and warns inexperienced trampers not to attempt the more dangerous sections of the track.

Sections of the track are quite often officially closed due to landslides, floods and other incidents, and would-be Rees-Dart trampers are advised to check the DOC website for current advisory notices pertaining to the Rees-Dart before heading in. To check conditions and advisory notices first is a good idea for all tramps, but especially so in this case.

The lower part of the Dart valley, looking toward the mountains, in frost and sunshine

Rees-Dart Upper Valley

One of the huts

Snow on the Rees Saddle

*Two images of the Dart Glacier and its terminal moraine,
from slightly different vantage points*

*Poled route up to the Cascade Saddle, which lies
between the Rees-Dart and Matukituki valleys*

*The lonesome Cascade Saddle Toilet (top); view down the West
Branch of the Matukituki Valley from the Cascade Sadd*

Back down to civilisation, or at least Muddy Creek carpark

CHAPTER THIRTY-FOUR
A Visitation at Paringa

New Zealand two-dollar coin showing the locally-rare
Kōtuku or White Heron, ardea

T ALKING of wild and endangered species which can sometimes become
tame and come in from the wilderness such as the kea, I recall how
in the summer of 2006 / 2007 I visited the Salmon Farm Café near Lake
Paringa, close to the Haast Pass in remote South Westland. At the café, we

could drink coffee and look out on ponds full of the farm's stock splashing about.

Earlier, I had caught a glimpse of the highly conspicuous yet seldom-seen white heron or kōtuku, which appears on the New Zealand two-dollar coin and is a by-word in Māori culture for all that is rare and special.

So rare is the kōtuku that it is thought that only 100 to 120 of them live in New Zealand at the present time, so that it is even more rare than the kakapō. Thankfully the kōtuku (*ardea alba modesta*) is not confined to New Zealand, and also lives in flocks of thousands in Australia and Asia, where it is known in English as the eastern great egret.

The closely related great egret of Europe and the Americas (*ardea alba*), almost identical in outward appearance to the kōtuku, is the symbol of the national Audubon Society in the United States, the nearest American equivalent to New Zealand's Royal Forest and Bird Protection Society.

Clearly, there is something inspiring about *ardea alba* and its variants wherever they appear.

The word egret comes from the French word for brush, and refers to a heron that develops fine plumes that catch the wind in the breeding season. Many egrets were endangered by plume hunting in Victorian times, when it was fashionable to attach feathers of various sorts to women's hair, hats and dresses, and the kōtuku was nearly wiped out by the practice after its sole breeding site was discovered in 1865. Apart from the impressiveness of the bird, this fact also explains why *ardea alba* became the symbol of the Audubon society. The society's first order of business upon foundation at the beginning of the twentieth century was to prevent egrets, and various other sorts of birds, from being exterminated for the sake of fashion.

Even so, it seems that the kōtuku has *always* been exceptionally rare in this country. Māori tradition held that in spite of its conspicuity you would see a kōtuku only once in your life. Adding to its cachet as the symbol of all things rare and exotic was the fact that it was the only bird in New Zealand that had absolutely white feathers all over.

I beheld a kōtuku at a great distance with my own eyes shortly beforehand on that trip, and was well satisfied: tick that one off the bucket list, in other words.

Well, I was sitting down at the Salmon Farm Café with some friends when with a great flapping noise a male kōtuku dropped straight out of the sky and landed on a table next to me, a large, upright bird with loose and lacy breeding plumes, also in white, that caught the wind and blew this way and that in the gentle breeze.

The kōtuku was blindingly white all over apart from its eyes, its bill and its legs, and impressive in the extreme when it extended its wings. The total impression was angelic, and we could hardly believe what we were seeing. But I suspect the kōtuku was more interested in the salmon, than bestowing any kind of blessing upon us!

And so, the kōtuku can belie its rarity these days, and so does the kea, which is confined to New Zealand.

CHAPTER THIRTY-FIVE

Caples/Greenstone Track

MORE BIRDS GALORE

*The Caples / Greenstone Track loops around the HP Ailsa
Mountains, the clearly defined massif west of Lake Wakatipu
in this view.* Source: Google Maps Terrain View, Map Data ©2017

Y OU'RE going to drown!' I had been in life-threatening situations before, but despite my tramping companion's anxiety, this wasn't one of them. It was a beautiful day hiking the Caples and Greenstone tracks near Queenstown and, although it had been drizzling the previous week, DOC had assured us that the water levels of the rivers on the track were fine.

Still, my companion, a wealthy American woman in her mid-sixties, was terrified of drowning in a river out in the wild. Her fears were amplified by a group of sheep farmers who had joined us on the track and were now winding her up with tales of flooded creeks which were supposedly 'just up the path'!

I had first met this American woman in the summer of 2013. She was a member of the Wakatipu Tramping Club at the time and, sharing this mutual interest, we decided to tramp the Caples/Greenstone together.

This moderately demanding tramp winds its way through the beautiful Caples and Greenstone Valleys, which are linked by the subalpine pass of McKellar Saddle, offering incredible views of the surrounding landscape. There is plenty of native wildlife on the track, and we were lucky enough to see falcons, kea, mōhua, and plenty of other birds.

The tracks can be hiked from either end, one near Kinloch and Glenorchy and the other at The Divide on Milford Road. The Divide also is one of the end points for the nearby Routeburn Track and many exhausted trampers are picked up there, although some choose to extend their hike and carry on through the Caples/Greenstone for an epic six to eight-day tramp.

With or without this extension onto the Routeburn, the Caples/ Greenstone is still a demanding four-day journey, one that my companion was thoroughly unprepared for. She'd only brought a light pack and cold food, and, having only done guided tramps before, was very inexperienced in the wild.

We drove up to Glenorchy in my car and began our tramp at the end of Greenstone Road with a hike of nine kilometres to the Mid Caples Hut, the first hut on the track. Armed with my map and assurances from DOC about the river levels, I was ready for a good tramp. However, my companion from the Wakatipu Tramping Club wasn't quite so ready. Maybe it was the cold food or maybe it was my soup, but she was unwell with irritable bowel syndrome throughout the whole tramp. It has to be said that there was not much in the way of facilities along the path. DOC suggests burying human waste at least 50 metres from tracks, huts and water sources. Thankfully there was little fear of contaminating the latter as, due to my colleague's fear of drowning, we stayed well away from water sources! From the Mid Caples Hut, it was a further two-hour hike up the valley to our first overnight stay at the old Upper Caples Hut, which is now managed and maintained by the New Zealand Deerstalkers Association.

While several huts on the Caples/Greenstone are privately owned, it is DOC who have done a lot of work on the track, seriously improving it from its origins as a pack track from Central Otago to the West Coast. The Greenstone Valley was first tramped by Māori in search of pounamu (greenstone), giving the valley its name. This stone was incredibly valuable for Māori as a material for weapons, tools and treasured objects. Tribes from around the area continued to undertake greenstone expeditions through the valley as late as 1850, when the first Europeans also began to explore the area.[82] One of these, a prospector named Patrick Caples, become the first European to reach the Tasman Sea from Wakatipu, returning via the valley which now bears his last name after a long three-month walk.

Caples Valley was first settled by farmers in 1880, and the Greenstone Valley nearby was used as a stock trail for several years before being developed into a track as the tourist trade took off. Although the track is managed by DOC as a public conservation area for the people of New Zealand, the surrounding land is largely owned by the Ngāi Tahu.[83] The valleys are mostly used for tramping, although there is some farmland in the area, and a lot of trapping is also done near the track.

After spending the night in the Upper Caples Hut, we carried on to the McKellar Hut, tramping around twenty-two kilometres between the huts through beech forests to reach Lake McKellar, near which the hut of the same name stands. Coming off McKellar Saddle, there was a beautiful view of Mount Christina just before we went down towards the lake.

It was along this stretch that my companion met the sheep farmers from the Christchurch area who started winding her up, telling her she was going to drown in the creek further up. I tried to set things straight, but she believed them over me despite their lack of experience on the track.

We made good time to McKellar Hut and checked in at 3.00 pm. All my colleague wanted to do was spend the rest of the day indoors, no doubt discouraged by all the talk of supposedly flooded rivers. Well, nothing could have bored me more! The whole reason I was tramping was to get outside and do things, not stay inside a hut. So, I left my companion with her new sheep farming friends and tried to carry on to Lake Mackenzie, which is about ten kilometres away from McKellar Hut.

The lake is part of the nearby Routeburn Track, and I happened to know the DOC warden there from my time volunteering with the organisation a few years earlier. However, I didn't manage to make it, and as the shadows started lengthening over the trees, I had to turn around and hope I could make it back to McKellar Hut before nightfall. I got back at eight p.m., only to find the farmers had upset my companion so much she was going to come looking for me, thinking I could have had an accident. She'd apparently said how unhappy she was with me for leaving her and taking that risk, but I told her there was no reason to be worried – the Routeburn is a Great Walk, not a backcountry track.

The atmosphere on the tramp was pretty stiff after that, but there was some other interesting company in the hut besides us and the devious farmers. I met an Israeli sergeant who was in charge of drone strikes in the Palestinian West Bank, and we got to talking about her life in the army. I made no judgement about her, but I had to speak up when she told me her troops, who were eighteen years old, had refused to fire on Palestinian teenagers. She said that she had trouble with her soldiers, and their concerned parents were always calling her to ask if they were OK. I told her that if her troops were anything like eighteen-year-old Kiwis, they could not cope with compulsory conscription or war. When you're eighteen you're still basically a child, and no parent should have to send their child into a warzone, whether it's compulsory or not.

After a good night's sleep in McKellar Hut, we had a reasonably uneventful eighteen-kilometre tramp to the Greenstone Hut where we next stopped. After that, it was another twelve-kilometre hike through the rest of the valley before we crossed the Caples River on a swing bridge and re-joined the Caples Track. From there it was another thirty minutes back to the carpark where we had started.

It had been quite the tramp, but I had enjoyed the wilderness and my companion had seen birds, which was good. Afterwards, though, she went back to the Wakatipu Tramping Club quite out of sorts. I was upset that she had chosen to believe a couple of sheep farmers she had just met over me, especially ones who had refused to pay the standard hut fee at McKellar.

Every now and then you have these troubles when you go tramping. So, when I want to go tramping to have a holiday and chill, I've decided it's actually better to do it by myself than with other people: so long as it is not somewhere too dangerous.

I visited the Caples/Greenstone again more recently, in 2016, this time hoping to tramp it solo. However, it was so overcrowded that I drove down to Lake Hauroko instead. Still, I suppose that was for the best, as the journey with the woman from the Wakatipu Tramping Club was really only the latest in a series of interesting experiences I've had on the Caples/Greenstone track.

Most notably, I was living there for a week as a temporary hut warden for DOC after the Wakatipu region decided they were going to take on volunteers. It seemed like a pretty straightforward, yet interesting, job, I thought – little knowing what I was truly in for: taking a crash course in plumbing and getting very, very bored.

It was also when I really got to know about some of the astonishing conditions the hut wardens have to work in. I met a Ngāi Tahu woman who told me that she and the other hut wardens worked week-on, week-off, and they only got paid for thirty hours. There was another lovely Japanese guy named Haitu (I think) who has worked on the Caples/Greenstone for years – and at thirty hours, they don't even get a liveable wage!

Unlike both of these salaried wardens, though, I had volunteered to be a DOC hut warden. I was assigned at this time to the Mid Caples Hut, which is the first stop on the track. It was a bit boring. The hut is surrounded by pasture and was only two hours into the tramp, so there wasn't a lot to see and not many trampers chose to stay there.

I took enough food in, but I ran out of bread and was at a bit of a loss as to how to replace it until I saw some of the locals who were out fishing in the streams. Because a fishing licence for two weeks is only $150, quite a few Australians come for a fishing holiday and stay in the huts on the Caples/

Greenstone tracks. However, a lot of them put the fish they catch back in the water because, apparently, the number they catch is unsustainable.

Catch-and-release past the bag limit is by no means 'victimless'; after all, the fish don't know they are going to be released, and the hook is painful. It's the equivalent of a well-fed cat playing with a mouse that it has no intention of eating. Anyhow, I didn't realise that was the practice and I naturally thought, 'Yum! Brown trout!' So, I cadged one that they were going to put back, boiled it up in the oven, had some for myself and gave the rest to the people in the hut. Brown trout are not native to New Zealand, in any case so it is not as if I was consuming an endangered species.

I had quite good people in the hut at the time, and thankfully only a few were messy. During the week there, I also really enjoyed meeting the other wardens in other huts along the track and making friends. Then I headed to the Upper Caples Hut, where I was told that the water had stopped and needed to be got running again. They seriously should have got a professional in for these issues – I mean, neither I nor the other wardens had any idea what we were doing when it came to plumbing! Or maybe trained us up to the point that we knew what we were doing.

I believe the Ngāi Tahu warden must have left because when I went back to the Caples/Greenstone a couple of years later, there was a rock climber from Australia there instead. Apparently in the Wakatipu region they are employing more people like him who have degrees in parks and recreation, but I think the best people are employed in the nearby Te Anau region, a plum posting which includes the prestigious Routeburn, Milford and Kepler Tracks, three of New Zealand's ten Great Walks.

On the Routeburn Track, close to where I was working on the Caples/Greenstone, I noticed that they tended to employ former police officers. Coming from a policing background they've dealt with trouble from disruptive young people before, and know how to look after older people too. I think this makes them the best hut wardens for busy tourist trails.

Wages and conditions vary depending on where you are. On the Routeburn the hut wardens are paid for a twelve-hour day and work six

The Caples Valley, carved out by broad Pleistocene glaciers and narrow modern streams

days a week before having six days off. While the wages are low, they are much better there than on the secondary tracks where I worked. Still, from both my own experiences and from talking to a friend of mine who works on the Routeburn Track, I've decided that being a hut warden really isn't easy wherever you are.

Caples Valley (top); Mount Christina from the McKellar Saddle (bottom)

Caples / Greenstone scenes including Upper Caples Hut

Out through the Greenstone, another 'big valley' from the
Pleistocene. I must have been quite tired by this stage.

CHAPTER THIRTY-SIX

Romance on the Routeburn

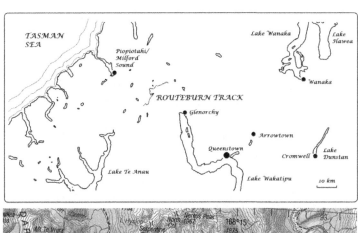

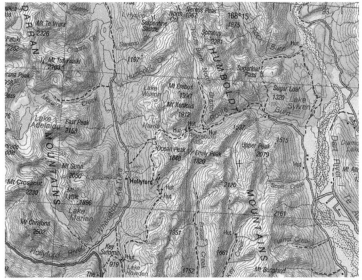

*The Routeburn Track through the Humboldt Mountains, showing
local relationships to Queenstown and Glenorchy, Darran
Mountains, Lake Marian and Dart River / Te Awa Whakatipu.*

Lower map LINZ via NZTopomaps.com

O NE of New Zealand's ten Great Walks is the Routeburn Track, which links the Mount Aspiring and Fiordland National Parks in South West New Zealand, the second of the two World Heritage Sites on the mainland islands of New Zealand (there is a third, offshore World Heritage Site in New Zealand, in remote sub-Antarctic islands which I have not yet visited).

In contrast to Tongariro National Park, which is deemed a landscape of outstanding natural *and* cultural significance, the World Heritage status of South West New Zealand and the sub-Antarctic islands is purely of the natural kind. This is not to say that it has no cultural significance at all, for in fact the region includes much of the Māori greenstone trail and the ultimate sources of the greenstone. But, officially, the United Nations has gazetted South West New Zealand for its natural qualities alone.

Only a short drive from Glenorchy, the Routeburn Track cuts through the Humboldt Mountains, a range named after the German geographer Alexander von Humboldt. Many geographical features in the more rugged parts of the South Island have German, Austrian or Swiss-sounding names, a reflection of the fact that several nineteenth-century explorers of the South Island and its mountains came from central Europe.

The Department of Conservation calls the Routeburn Track 'the ultimate alpine adventure'.[84] In the warmer part of the year, the Great Walk season, the adventure consists of a 32-km tramp through bush below the treeline and through alpine meadows in which mountain flowers such as South Island Edelweiss are often in bloom. Named, no doubt, by the aforementioned explorers, South Island Edelweiss are unrelated to the original Edelweiss of Europe, but they look similar. Other alpine flowers of the South Island include numerous species of large daisies and the Mount Cook Lily, misnamed because it is actually a buttercup. As an alpine adventure, the

Routeburn Track boasts unrivalled views of the Southern Alps to the east and the Darran Mountains to the west.

The Routeburn Track is a very popular walk and must be booked well in advance if you go during the Great Walk season, which technically extends from Labour Weekend, the fourth weekend of October – a holiday which honours the toiler, in a similar fashion to Mothers' Day – until 27 April. Although the huts often fill up fast, there are also several campsites in scenic locations near the huts for those wishing to camp outside, although this is best during the warmer months. These campsites are much needed, too, because in recent years the tracks have become really full as tourists have flocked to the Routeburn and other Great Walks over summer.

One reason for the Routeburn's popularity could be its abundance of appearances in films. The mountains behind nearby Glenorchy, mountains which can be viewed from the start of the track, were used as the location of the Misty Mountains in the *Lord of the Rings*.[85] Other sections near the track were also used in its prequel, *The Hobbit*. Air New Zealand also used the Routeburn as a set for an airline safety video with *Man vs Wild* star Bear Grylls, who was quick to heap praises on the track, calling it "one of the most beautiful places on Earth."[86] Trampers seem to agree, with an estimated 13,000 visiting the track every year.[87]

Wanting to see what the all the fuss was about, I tramped the Routeburn with two friends from Auckland. Both my friends were great fun to tramp with and took some amazing photos along the way, especially of Mount Christina and the Hollyford Mountains.

Like the nearby Caples/Greenstone, the Routeburn can be started at either end of the track; beginning at the Divide, which is one and a half hours from Te Anau, or the Routeburn Shelter, which is a 68-km drive from Queenstown along the banks of Lake Wakatipu, near the small town of Glenorchy. Much of this area resembles the Scottish Highlands, whence names like Glenorchy. Lake Wakatipu is the local version of Loch Ness, complete with a monster whose slow heartbeat explained a regular, if slight, rising and falling of the waters to the Māori who prospected for greenstone in the area. Modern scientists, spoilsports that they are, say it is a consequence of winds blowing up and down the lake.

We caught a lift to the Divide and began our tramp with a hike of just under nine kilometres between the Routeburn Shelter and the Routeburn Falls Hut, where there is a spectacular waterfall. From there, we carried on to Lake Mackenzie Hut for the second-longest section of the track, hiking a bit over eleven kilometres through the valley and up over the Harris Saddle. The Saddle is the highest point on the track at 1,225 metres and offers expansive views of the valley and the nearby Darran Mountains. I saw rock wren there, which nest on the track in summer, and Murray took some amazing photos of the kea on the track.

From the Harris Saddle, we descended along the exposed Hollyford Face towards Lake Mackenzie Hut, where we stayed overnight before carrying on to complete the last section of the Routeburn. This final stretch was a twelve-kilometre hike past the impressive Earland Falls and humble Lake Howden Hut to reach the Divide and finish our tramp. Leaving the Lake Mackenzie area was hard, though, as it was here near the end our tramp that I made friends with a DOC warden named Evan. Despite the DOC hut being an unlikely setting for romance, we really connected and ended up together for about four months.

Evan was one of the longest-standing wardens on the Routeburn, as both he and his friend Clive had thirty-five years of experience between them on the track. Over Christmas and New Year, they host what's known as the 'Highland Games', with Christmas cake and all sorts of pole-vaulting games.

This event attracted a lot of media attention, and Clive was interviewed on National Radio about it. As a result, the Routeburn Track is always full over Christmas time with trampers flocking to join the festivities.

The two wardens shared a small hut near Mackenzie Hut which has become like a home to them. At one stage DOC was threatening to reduce their hours, and in protest Evan and Clive were going to empty out their hut and leave. They'd prepared to helicopter all their stuff out and then walk out, but thankfully DOC realised they were worth keeping on and increased both their hours and their pay. I think that was fair enough, too, because people who have 35 years of experience between them should be paid more than $16 an hour.

A pay rise should also be merited when you consider that DOC wardens have to work hard just to keep their tracks open! In winter, sections of the Routeburn suffer from avalanches which DOC try to control by letting off charges to clear them – I found out that Evan had had to take a dynamiting course to learn how to do this safely.

The snow risk is quite high on the Routeburn, and one year a group were even snowed in over Christmas and had to be helicoptered from the Routeburn Falls Hut to Mackenzie Hut, as the Harris Saddle was impassable. In fact, white Christmases are very common in all inland and elevated parts of New Zealand, even though Christmas is the middle of summer (theoretically speaking). I say theoretically speaking, for there is often an unseasonal cold snap around what is, for us, the summer solstice. Every New Zealander knows that winter has not truly given up its lease until that Christmas cold snap has been and gone.

For instance, Christmas Day in 1975 was exceptionally cold and it snowed in many upland areas. I believe snow was even seen in the North

Island town of Dannevirke, a Scandinavian settlement by no means alpine in nature. It must have seemed just like the old country.

As I have mentioned in *A Maverick Traveller*, all of this happens because New Zealand's climate is unusually oceanic and exposed, just like New Zealand itself, with no great continental land-mass to produce reliable summer heat. In fact, it often seems as though the weather in New Zealand depends less on the time of year than the direction from which the wind is blowing. This is not all a bad thing by any means: it means that summers are usually not *too* dry or hot and also that, just like summer snow, hot bikini days in the middle of winter are occasionally enjoyed.

Altogether, 'four seasons in one day' is perhaps the commonest of New Zealand idioms. But what this also means that you can never be complacent in the New Zealand outdoors, no matter where you are and no matter the time of year.

During past Great Walks seasons, if an avalanche has blocked the track, helicopter rides to the next hut have been offered to trampers at a price.

When they're not blowing away snow throughout the year to keep the avalanche risk down, both Evan and Clive also have to clear the windfall, the native bush that falls down at the beginning of the season. There is a lot of skill involved in being a DOC warden, as you have to have mountaineering experience, explosives training, and all sorts of other skills.

Despite these dangers, it's no wonder Evan and Clive have been on the Routeburn for so long, as this beautiful part of the country is really hard to leave! The views are breath-taking and its valleys are steeped in history, having been tramped for centuries, first by Māori for pounamu and then by prospectors for gold.[88] Today, the value of the track isn't in gold or greenstone but in the journey itself.

The Routeburn really is a beautiful spot for either romance or a great walk, and I was quite lucky to get both when I tramped it.

(I am grateful to Murray Green for several of the photographs used in this chapter.)

Amazing blue, clear water on the Routeburn Track;
the Sabine River in Nelson is like this too

Flowers and pathways on the Routeburn Track

Looking down onto the Routeburn Flats

Alpine flowers (top); Darran Mountains from Harris Saddle (bottom)

Mount Christina (top); Routeburn Falls Hut area (bottom)

Harris Saddle and Lake Harris

Harris Saddle and Lake Harris, view from on high

Kea

*Fantail with
eyes glowing
in flash.*

Harris Saddle

Lake Mackenzie

Vicinity of Lake Mackenzie (top); camping flat area (bottom)

CHAPTER THIRTY-SEVEN

Kepler Track

JUST DIVINE VIEWS

The Kepler Track, a loop between Lake Te Anau (top right) and Lake Manapouri. From *Kepler Track* (brochure), Wellington, Department of Conservation, September 2016

THE Kepler Track begins on the shores of the sprawling Lake Te Anau – the largest body of fresh water in the South Island of New Zealand – and winds its way through the spectacular Fiordland National Park. Traversing sixty kilometres up alpine heights and alongside two beautiful lakes, the track, which is circular in form, starts and ends only five kilometres from the town of Te Anau, itself not far from Queenstown.

One of New Zealand's Great Walks, the Kepler Track was constructed in 1988 to take some of the pressure off the busy Milford and Routeburn tracks, but soon became popular in its own right. The Kepler normally requires bookings during the Great Walks season (October-April), but when I went to tramp it, it was actually completely full and so the only way to tramp it was to start in the opposite direction to usual.

It was 2006 and I went with two others to Te Anau, although only two of us would tramp the Kepler Track. The track itself follows a loop from the Kepler carpark and, although you can walk both ways, most trampers start off tramping to the Luxmore Hut high above Lake Te Anau. Because the huts were full, we had to start off our tramp heading in the opposite direction, hiking towards Rainbow Reach carpark and onwards to our first stop at Moturau Hut on the shores of Lake Manapouri.

We left at two p.m. and tramped nine and a half kilometres to the carpark at Rainbow Reach, which took us around two and a half hours. From there we crossed the Waiau River on a swing bridge and carried on for six kilometres up the track towards Moturau Hut, where the hut warden was waiting for us. From the Kepler carpark, it had taken us around five hours to reach the hut, walking alongside the river's edge and through a swampy area of wetlands.

The Moturau Hut was quite dirty inside, and we saw kea outside the hut pulling out the nails. These mischievous birds are very curious and as well as attacking the odd car tyre, they enjoy pulling nails out of buildings with their beaks. However, the lead in old-fashioned roof nails kills kea, and along with possums, lead poisoning is becoming quite a threat to this protected species – so much so that DOC made an effort to replace all the lead-headed roof nails in their huts with modern, unleaded ones.

The Kepler Track, with views of the Murchison Mountains and Lake Te Anau

After spending the night in Moturau, we tramped onwards towards Iris Burn Hut. It was a long stretch of a little over sixteen kilometres between these two huts, heading uphill through beech forest and a winding gorge for around five to six hours. At Iris Burn we met a group of ex-army women and men who were camping out, and I heard kiwi calling out in the bush at night. That was really unusual because we were told that kiwi are dying out. From Iris Burn Hut we got some really beautiful views of the Kepler Track, which only became more impressive as we tramped the five to six-hour walk, a bit under fifteen kilometres, to our next stop at Luxmore Hut. This route takes you up along a ridge just under Mt Luxmore, which has stunning views of Lake Te Anau and the Murchison Mountains.

The route down the mountain leads to Brod Bay campsite on the shores of Lake Te Anau, a distance of a bit over eight kilometres, and from there it was only a short one and a half hour walk back to the Kepler carpark where we had started.

CHAPTER THIRTY-EIGHT

Lake Marian

CAMPING AND LOOKING AT THE ROUTEBURN

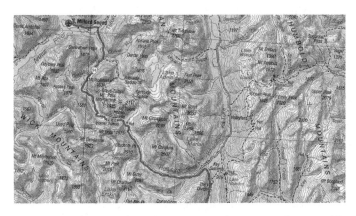

Map above shows Lake Marian in wider region from Milford Sound to Humboldt Mountains. Map below shows Lake Marian at lower left in more detail, between the Darran and Ailsa Mountains. The Hollyford Valley is in the middle of both maps.
(LINZ via NZTopomaps.com)

Lake Marian in Fiordland National Park is more than a little off the beaten path in some ways since the nearest main road is the one that leads to Milford Sound. Yet it is accessible in others, since it is not far from the main road to Milford Sound and yet it lies in an alpine wilderness that seems as though it should be remote from any road.

Located southwest of Gunn's Camp in the Hollyford Valley, the track to the lake begins from Marian Carpark, one kilometre down the unsealed Hollyford Road from its intersection with the main road leading to Milford Sound, some ninety kilometres out from Te Anau.

Part of the larger Fiordland National Park, which was declared a protected area in 1952, the Lake Marian Track is often overlooked by the thousands of visitors who flock to the area. This is in spite of its incredible alpine features.[89] While the remote back-country hike beyond the lake is recommended for advanced trampers only, the track to the lake is only a two to four-hour return trip from the Marian carpark – although most stay longer for the photo opportunities!

I have been to Lake Marian twice. The first time was when I hiked up there with my brother, who was very stressed out with his work in Thames so I thought the outdoors would be good for him. After leaving the car-park, we crossed a swing bridge and continued on to the spectacular Marian Falls, which are only ten minutes down the track. The track had been washed out in places by the rain. Between flooding and the windfall from the bush, I'm sure the park rangers often have to clear the track. When we reached the lake, we saw a party of ten locals who had tramped up with plastic kayaks, blown them up and were kayaking on the lake, which was pretty cool! We had a lot of fun posing on rocks by the lake, and then tramped back down.

The next time I went to Lake Marian was with my friend Jean-Claude, who is introduced in *A Maverick Traveller*. Jean-Claude and I also tried to get up to Mt Aspiring, but that's another story. We camped overnight by Lake Marian and it was beautiful. Our boots were wet so we dried them over a campfire, which Jean-Claude was very good at (as you might expect it is important get them neither too close, nor too far). Overnight, there were no sounds of birds – not even one kea call. The population of these cheeky alpine parrots is in decline nationally.[90] Their main predator is possums and though I'm not sure if possums survive in snow, I do believe I've seen possums around the bush line. So, this definitely shows a reason for the decline of the kea, apart from them ripping out leaded nails from huts, which is surely a secondary issue.

After Lake Marian I was going to do a tramp over to Lake Adelaide which is nearby, but I really don't like the walkwires, or two-wire bridges (one for your feet, one for your hands) which are strung out over the rivers there. Generally, my pack is so heavy that I'm not very balanced. If I have to cross these walkwires, I'd rather do it with a group than on my own. I usually prefer to tramp through rivers because I feel safer with my feet on the ground. There are many walkwires around this area of the Fiordland National Park and I try to avoid them, although even they seem infinitely safer than the bridges I encountered in Nepal which were *full* of holes!

*Getting in to Lake
Marian with my
brother Lawrie*

Lake Marian, looking toward the Darran Mountains in Fiordland

At the Lake

At Lake Marian, looking toward the Ailsa Mountains where the Routeburn Track is (top) and toward the Darran Mountains (middle and bottom).

391

CHAPTER THIRTY-NINE

Homer Hut / Gertrude Saddle

A ROCK CLIMBER'S PARADISE

Gertrude Saddle at centre top. Lake Marian bottom right, state highway to Milford also visible (Cleddau Valley, Homer Tunnel and Upper Hollyford Valley). (LINZ via NZTopomaps.com)

I HAD an adventure of quite a different kind when I went tramping and climbing in the Gertrude Valley in the Fiordland National Park. Nestled underneath the Darran Mountain Range, the valley is reached from a carpark that turns off Milford Road almost one hundred kilometres from Te Anau. The road turns off just before the Homer Tunnel entrance, about ten kilometres past the turnoff to Hollyford Road at Marian Corner which leads to the Lake Marian Track. While exploring the area, I went to Homer Hut with my sister who was taking photos. It was filled with rock climbers so we stayed in a tent outside the modest Homer Hut right at the start of

393

the Gertrude Saddle Track, which lies just behind the carpark down a short access road. This hut is owned by the New Zealand Alpine Club and is a simple, functional place with thirty bunk beds and no showers. It was built in the early 1960s by the club and opened in 1965, continuing to operate for forty years before being refurbished in the summer of 2005–06.[91] Despite being deep in the Fiordland National Park, Homer Hut is actually looked after by a guy in Invercargill called Steve Walker. The New Zealand Alpine Club has many dedicated members like Steve who look after their huts, which is becoming very important with DOC pulling out of maintaining the huts. Often when this happens, a person will adopt a hut and become responsible for its maintenance just to stop it from falling into disrepair.

Many rock climbers tend to stay at Homer Hut because the nearby Darran Mountain Range is a great area for rock-climbing. With the proximity of the hut to Mount Talbot, Mount Crosscut and Mount Moir, climbers have plenty of options for one-day trips, or can venture further into the mountain range for longer climbing trips such as the guided five-day North Buttress of Sabre, or the overnight climb to Mitre Peak. Some of the more well-known short climbs in the valley are on the south face of Mount Moir, known as Moir's Mate, where there are popular crags such as the Bowen Allan Corner, which was first climbed in 1972 by Stu Allan and John Bowen.[92] Other routes, such as the Lucky Strike on the west face of Moir's Mate, have only been mapped out in more recent times. There are still plenty of places in these wild mountains for ambitious climbers to carve their own routes. There are also some famous rock climbers who come here to climb the lofty peaks of the Darran Mountains.

While at the Homer Hut, I tried rock climbing and bouldering, which is when you climb around a boulder rather than up a rock wall. I met a climber by the name of Paul Rogers who had put the bolts on some of the rock walls in the 1980s, a pioneering feat which would have taken a lot of work.

I had previously tried to rock climb outside of Queenstown in a place called Gorge Road, and also at Wye Creek, a rock climbing nirvana about twenty minutes' drive from Queenstown. This spectacular area offers beautiful views of the Queenstown area. There is also a walking track nearby where people take their dogs and then go climbing. I am not a rock climber, but I love freedom climbing with my pack and I've navigated some quite dangerous areas while up in the mountains. I think women generally underestimate their abilities as to what they can do. Still, I'm just a beginner and I need to find a partner who would be interested in climbing with me. I think after all these years I might have finally found somebody to be my climbing partner who is the same age and level of ability as me. We're not as fit as twenty-five-year-olds but there's something about finding a good climbing partner which helps you get into it a bit more.

My sister and I went up the Gertrude Saddle, which is quite a hard walk through the valley and up steep rock slabs and boulders. But it's very picturesque so we had to pause for a few photo breaks. It's about a five-hour or seven-kilometre return trip and, when you reach the top of the mountain, you get a beautiful view of Mountain's Bay, the Gertrude Valley and part of Milford Sound/Piopiotahi.

On the way up, we met a group of young native Americans who had brought an American flag with them to take photos with, one they said symbolised the Iroquois nation, not the USA. It wasn't a conventional view of the flag, so they taught us a few things. As we climbed up, it became slippery and icy and I slipped and fell on my kneecap. It was not an easy hike and, when I think about it, I was lucky not to have broken my kneecap. The American boys helped me up to the top, and I got a photo taken with them and their flag. They were a little bit coy at first and asked, 'Do you mind having a photo taken under the US flag?' But I didn't mind at all.

I love Homer Hut and the Gertrude Valley and have been out there about five times. One of the more recent times was about two years ago, when I got the wrong date for an ice climbing weekend. I had read that the Ice Climbing Festival was 10–18 July, but for some strange reason I went down on the twentieth of July. I was so stressed out about something so I got the wrong date and spent the night at Homer Hut by myself. It was fantastic; the hut was full of wood and coal so I had a blazing fire and there was a full moon out as well. I really enjoyed myself. I've also been there in the winter and taken my Subaru four-wheel drive down with snow tyres attached so I can drive over the snow to the hut. It really is beautiful in winter and I do need to make a return visit soon.

Gertrude Saddle

Gertrude Saddle

CHAPTER FORTY

Hollyford Track

WHERE THE HUNTERS FEED YOU VENISON

*The Hollyford Track Area. The Track goes down the lower Hollyford Valley
and around the coastal Skippers Range.* (LINZ via NZTopomaps.com)

I T was April/May 2012 and, fresh from the summer tramping season, I decided to hike the beautiful Hollyford Track in the Fiordland National Park. It was an epic four-day journey with a pre-booked jetboat ride back to a lake near the start of the track to shorten the return trip, which is not an option so readily available on most of the other tramps I'd done in New Zealand. I tramped the nine kilometres up from Lower Hollyford Road to the beautiful Hidden Falls, a walk of about two to three hours, and went on the nearby Pyke River swing bridge, which is the longest swing bridge in the National Park. I spent the night there at the Hidden Falls Hut, and woke early to see a beautiful low-lying fog blanketing the valley – what a majestic sight for only my second day on the Hollyford!

Following the path of a long-gone glacier, the Hollyford Valley cuts its way through the Darran Mountain area and out to the Tasman Sea, encompassing much of New Zealand's natural beauty in one walk. Unlike nearby tracks which close occasionally through autumn and winter due to avalanche risks, landslides and the like, the Hollyford Valley is a low-altitude 'flat walk' and can be walked all year round. Like many other tracks in the Fiordland National Park, Hollyford was first used by the Ngāi Tahu Māori as an ancient greenstone trail, and later as an important mahinga kai (food gathering site). The Hollyford River which runs down the valley has an official Māori name, the Whakatipu Kā Tuku, a name that once again refers to the huge mountain lake on which all local life centred in pre-European times just as it does today. A waka (canoe) building site was also established around Lake Alabaster, or Wāwāhi Waka, as the Māori called it.

Later it was farmed by European settlers, including one named Davey Gunn who had his own rich history in the valley:

In 1926, [Gunn] first rode over the Greenstone Track to the Hollyford Valley where he would spend much of the rest of his life. He initially ran cattle in the area… but during the mid-1930s decided to branch out into tourism. Gunn built several huts which he charged out to trampers at twelve shillings and six dimes per day and provided guides at an extra pound a day. In 1936, he led his first party of 12 trampers over the Hollyford Track. To avoid the notorious Demon Trail around Lake McKerrow, Gunn took them across the lake in his launch, and elsewhere provided horses for those who wanted to ride.[93]

Gunn's legacy can be seen on the trail at the excellent Martins Bay, Hidden Falls and Deadman's huts which he built, along with Gunn's Camp further up the valley, which I was to visit after I had tramped the Hollyford.

At Hidden Falls Hut, where I'd stayed the night, it was the 'Roar' (deer mating season) – so called because you could hear all the stags roaring to attract the does. There were plenty of hunters out in the Hollyford Valley at the time, and I had heard stories of irresponsible ones shooting deer on the track just outside the hut sending stray bullets whizzing far too close to unwary trampers. They must have been just stories though, because I had only good experiences of hunters during my walk, and found most of them to be very considerate.

I left Hidden Falls and tramped around ten kilometres to the fork where the track splits off into the Demon Trail heading towards Martins Bay, or the Pyke-Big Bay Route which heads through to Olivine Hut. I dumped my pack at the fork and took a detour up the beginning of the Big Bay Route to see Lake Alabaster and the Alabaster Hut. It was pretty rustic and quaint but looked lovely.

I also checked out the privately-owned Pyke Lodge, one of the Ultimate Hikes huts which offer trampers gourmet food and all the comforts of home. I met a man working there as a guide who said he just couldn't wait to leave. I've heard this from quite a number of people who work extremely long hours at these lodges where they virtually have to do everything. They have to cook, guide walks, organise luggage and make sure the food comes in – it is an extremely hard job, so no wonder this man had had enough.

I saw Conservation Point, then I went back to pick up my pack and carry on to McKerrow Island Hut on the Demon Trail, which is a ten-and-a-half-kilometre hike from Lake Alabaster and takes about three to four hours. I spent my second night on the Hollyford here and met a tramper who was fishing in Lake McKerrow because he'd run out of food!

I enjoyed my time at this beautiful hut and the next day headed towards Hokuri Hut, which was around fourteen kilometres away. An hour and a half into the walk I stopped off at Demon Trail Hut for a short break when I saw some surviving kaka, a rare native parrot that was breeding in and around the trees near the hut. After this hut, the track got very steep and full of knotted tree roots, which was quite a challenge. It was cloudy above the Demon Trail and I could imagine that when it rained the track would become incredibly slippery. The track was also intercut with the many creeks which flow into Lake McKerrow, all with walkwires strung out across them so that trampers that can ford them safely.

I stayed in the Hokuri Hut that night and went to explore nearby Jamestown. This fascinating place was established in the late 1860s in an attempt to expand the frontiers of Greater Otago by building a new town on the coast near Martins Bay. While the creator of the town, James Macandrew (whom it was named after) thought that it would be able to spread for miles around, the land was inhospitable and the first settlers struggled to make ends meet. Despite a road being promised them, it was never built, and the town was effectively cut off from the outside world when the shipping service to the bay stopped in the 1870s.[94] By 1879, the town was largely abandoned, and sank into disrepair, although a few homes were kept and passed down through families. These private sections are still there, and there are many who want a continuation of the road all the way through to from Lake Wakatipu to Martins Bay.

While essentially a ghost town now, Jamestown was an incredible place to visit. I left completely in awe after walking underneath the beautiful rimu trees there which are at least 1,500 years old.

After visiting Jamestown, I carried on through to Martins Bay Hut out on the coast, which is a thirteen-kilometre hike from Hokuri Hut and takes about four to five hours to complete. At Martins Bay Hut, there were some deer hunters from Te Anau and Queenstown who had cleaned up the hut and got rid of all the mice by drowning them in a trap made out of a wine bottle. I thought that was pretty amazing and learnt the technique from them, little knowing I would later use it in the Tablelands when I was a DOC warden in the Nelson area.

The hunters had used a helicopter to fly all their food in, and when two American guys arrived with only cold food, they offered them some venison. While they didn't take the offer, I was only too happy to oblige and the generous hunters ended up giving me a full meal with roast vegetables and cheese sauce – they even gave me dessert!

I stayed at Martins Bay for two nights, where I was completely taken by the beautiful area. I walked around the area and saw fur seals and the Tasman Sea, and overall felt that I had one up on *Castaway*!

I was to take the jet boat out, but found out they couldn't take me all the way to the end of Lake McKerrow because there had been a drought that year and the river levels were really low. There was another woman on the boat whom I didn't envy at all: a relief guide with two clients, a Spanish cigar-smoking man in his forties with a young South American girl of nineteen years old. The Spaniard was complaining about his sore muscles, which was a bit strange because I thought most people would know you have to prepare for tramping by exercising beforehand.

We were dropped off back onto the Demon Trail when the boat could go no further, and the South American immediately started moaning about having to walk on the 'awful-looking' tree roots. I heard the guide offer to carry the Spanish man's pack and tell them they'd only walk as far as they could – but still, it was a thirty-kilometre walk for them to the nearest hut, quite a long walk for one day! I had thought the boat was going to take us as far as Lake Alabaster, so it was quite a long walk for me as well considering I had had to walk to the boat and then to the next hut. Still, thirty kilometres in a day didn't faze me, but I felt extremely sorry for the guide with her two unfit clients.

Hollyford Valley

Hollyford Valley

Hollyford Valley

Hollyford Valley

Hollyford Valley

CHAPTER FORTY-ONE

Gunn's Camp (at Hollyford)

SMALL CABINS WITH FIREPLACES

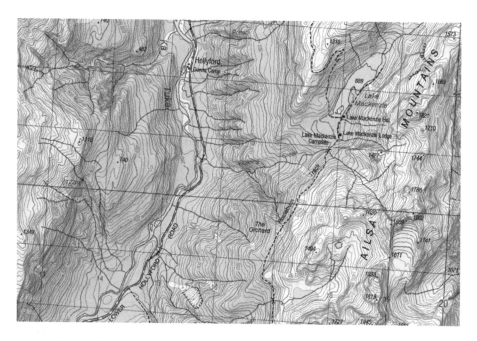

*Gunns Camp at top, at the Hollyford Locality, showin in relation
to the Ailsa Mountains, Lake Mackenzie and the Routeburn Track.*
(LINZ via NZTopomaps.com)

Aᴀꜰᴛᴇʀ I finished the Hollyford Track, I continued further down the
Hollyford Valley, heading inland to Gunn's Camp. From Milford
Highway, a right turn just past Main Divide leads into the valley via Lower
Hollyford Road. The historic campsite is eight kilometres down the dirt
road. A selection of rustic huts in a tranquil valley setting, Gunn's Camp

411

has a long history stretching back to 1938 where it began life as a temporary camp built to accommodate men working on the Hollyford-Okuru Road.[95] However, after the men left to fight in WWII, the road construction was abandoned. There are still signs up at Gunn's Camp that call for its continuation and for the government to fully link the Hollyford Valley to Te Anau and the Milford Sound.

After the war, the camp was plundered by holiday-makers in the late 1940s for building supplies, and when Davey Gunn bought it in 1950, there were only fifteen of the twenty-five original cabins remaining. Gunn had big plans for the area as a base for his tourism ventures and set about rebuilding the camp while pioneering guided walking and riding trips around Gunn's Camp and into the Hollyford Valley Track.

When Davey Gunn drowned in a creek on the Hollyford Track in 1955, his son, Murray Gunn, took over the camp and started a museum in honour of his father and other pioneers of the area.[96] Murray ran the camp and museum until his retirement in 2005, and management was taken over by the Hollyford Museum Charitable Trust. During my stay there, I met some of the members of this trust who were managing the huts and I really enjoyed talking to them. They stayed there for two weeks on and two weeks off, and most of them loved it. They weren't paid a lot of money, but were ardent lovers of the environment and apparently could save quite a bit – which is no wonder, considering the isolation of the camp!

It was the first time I'd ever stayed at Gunn's Camp and the whole place just blew me away. The camp has about twenty lovely camp cottages there that had been built by Davey Gunn. They all had beautiful little fireplaces in them and would be very cosy during winter. I was amazed by how they lit the hot water for the showers with an ingenious heating system made of a huge improvised water heater warmed by a blazing wood fire. After a long few days of tramping, having a hot shower again was great!

As well as hot water, they also have a single petrol pump which sells fuel at a steep price to cover the additional cost and inconvenience of pumping petrol at such a remote location. You can only purchase enough to get you to nearby Te Anau where you can properly refuel. The old pump has been at the campground since the 1920s or 1930s, but is now only used for emergencies.

Huts at Gunn's Camp

One of the cabins
at Gunn's Camp

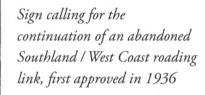

Sign calling for the
continuation of an abandoned
Southland / West Coast roading
link, first approved in 1936

The petrol pump

Gunn's Camp. Source: http://gunnscamp.org.nz

CHAPTER FORTY-TWO

Tramping the Milford Track and Feeling Very Scottish

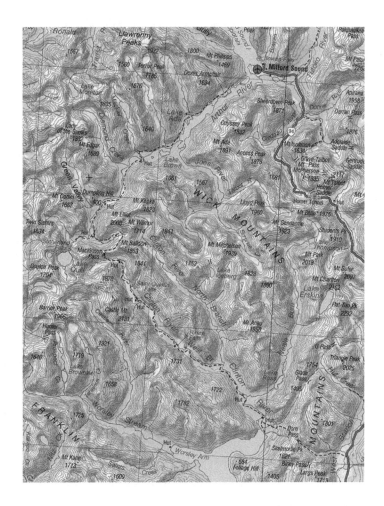

The Milford Track, normally accessed via a boat service on Lake Te Anau (at bottom), runs up the Clinton River, through the McKinnon Pass and down the Arthur River to Milford Sound. (LINZ via NZTopomaps.com)

415

I DID the Milford Track a few years ago with the Wakatipu Tramping Club after the end of the Great Walks season (October-April) when hut bookings are no longer required. The time between 27 April and the end of May is when a lot of locals do the walks because there's still coal and wood left in the huts.

It was the second tramp I'd been on with the Wakatipu Tramping Club to the Milford Sound area, the first being the Earnslaw Burn Track, which heads towards Mt Earnslaw/Pikirakatahi. On that one, the leader of the tramp turned out to be so unfit that he ended up at the back of the group and someone else had to take over as the leader. It's important to judge fitness correctly and as a general rule anything more than a day-walk requires a fair degree of fitness. All the same, I would say that the Milford Track is a relatively easy-to-medium tramp.

Doing the Milford Track, we got to Te Anau where we stayed at a motor camp and had to catch a boat the next morning at Te Anau Downs, about a 45-minute drive from the town. Te Anau is a very interesting place, with only two thousand permanent residents. I know the town very well because I go there periodically to buy wild venison, which is $30 a kilo. Nestled on the eastern shores of Lake Te Anau, the township of Te Anau is a very popular tourist destination because of its proximity to Milford Sound, the Kepler Track and other spectacular walks. However, it does have a 'shoulder season' – a period before the high numbers of travellers start to come in when the town is quieter. (With increasing tourism numbers this shoulder season may disappear.) The locals say that the clouds hover over the lake for the entire winter and that's why depression is reasonably common. While we don't usually have that in Wanaka or Queenstown, I remember there was a season around three years ago, when there were more clouds than sunlight and people were more affected by depression.

The town has a wonderful movie theatre called the Fiordland Cinema, which was especially constructed for the locally-filmed movie *Ata Whenua – Shadowland*. For reasons that I have just mentioned, Ata Whenua, meaning Shadowland, is the Māori name for the region, This film was directed by the recently deceased Dave Comer, who also worked on the *Lord of the Rings* trilogy as a location scout, and it was made to promote an understanding of Fiordland by exploring the Doubtful Sounds and the Southern Alps by air. As well as directing the film, Comer helped build the theatre to show his film because that was the only way he could promote it. Tourists from all over the place come to Te Anau to see the film, and it really is amazing.

With the current high levels of tourism in Queenstown, I think there's definitely going to be a spill-over into the nearby towns and I can see Te Anau becoming busier than it currently is. Wanaka and Queenstown really can't handle the accommodation crisis where lower-income workers and families are struggling to find housing because of the high prices which are driven up by seasonal tourism. Then again, you can build a lot of houses and end up making no money when the market goes down, though I don't think it's going to anytime soon.

The boat ride from Te Anau Downs was a lot of fun and the scenery around Lake Te Anau looked incredible from out in the water. It was bright outside so I wore my funny glasses which remind me of Bart Simpson. When I did the Mt Cook High Alpine Training Course, I had a white pair in the shape of hearts just for a bit of fun. We landed at Glade Wharf after about an hour on the boat and took a very nice introductory walk of about an hour to Clinton Hut, which is five kilometres from the wharf.

Anyway, there weren't any DOC wardens at Clinton Hut, or most of the huts on the track, for that matter. I think not having wardens in the off-season is an unfortunate cost-cutting measure by DOC and there should be at least one warden in the huts on the Great Walks during the off-season. Even overseas visitors know they can just walk in without paying even though they are supposed to have a backcountry hut pass or tickets which are $15 a night. Having a warden on would keep the money coming in and cover all the necessary expenses of maintaining the tracks and huts. People shouldn't be coming to New Zealand and using our facilities for absolutely nothing.

From Clinton Hut we tramped on towards Mintaro Hut, following the Clinton River sixteen and a half kilometres to Lake Mintaro in a walk that took us around six hours. The track got steeper from there as we climbed up towards the beautiful Mackinnon Pass, the highest point on the track, which has a real Scottish-highlands feel to it. Here we stopped to take in the incredible views and see the memorial to Quintin McKinnon who, with his friend Earnest Mitchell, discovered the route from Te Anau to the Milford Sound in 1888 and slashed out the track through the dense Fiordland forest.[97] I loved the Mackinnon Pass and even though it was cloudy the view of the entire mountain range was really impressive. The pass has its own beauty and I can see why people are attracted to it. We tramped downhill from here to Dumpling Hut, which is fourteen kilometres (six to seven hours) from Mintaro Hut.

Our tramp between these two huts ended up taking a little longer because we left the track to visit the magnificent Sutherland Falls, which are the highest waterfalls in New Zealand, and were only a one and a half hour-return tramp from the main track. However, when we reached the turnoff at the Quintin Shelter, we found it was taped off because there was work to be done on the track.

We all wanted to see the falls, so we went over the taped-off area in complete disregard for health and safety. While we made it to the waterfalls, we were caught on the way back by a DOC officer. An elderly member of the tramping club, who was a lovely guy, said he suffered from dementia and couldn't read the signs. Because this came from a dear old man, the DOC warden cracked up, but after she finished laughing she was really serious and gave us a right talking to.

After our adventure at Sutherland Falls, we continued on to Dumpling Hut where we spent the night. Our final day on the Milford Track was the eighteen-kilometre tramp to Sandfly Point, passing the impressive Mackay Falls near the Arthur River, and the equally mesmerising Giant Gate Falls beside Lake Ada. At Sandfly Point, the track runs into the Milford Sound and from the bay you can see the magnificent Mitre Peak rising over the fiord. As we caught a short boat ride past Mitre Peak to finish our tramp, it wasn't hard to see why it is perhaps the most iconic mountain in New Zealand.

As well as my tramp with the Wakatipu Tramping Club, I have been in the Milford Sound area on numerous other occasions. I generally stay at the Milford Sound Backpackers which is a fifteen-minute walk from the lakefront in Te Anau, and is absolutely beautiful. It's fantastic that people from many countries want to know about the area, and for first-time visitors I would highly recommend taking a boat ride through Milford Sound as well.

Milford Sound – Mitre Peak in the middle is
1,690 metres high, more than a mile

The Milford Track

The boat to the start of the Milford Track from Te Anau Downs, on Lake Te Anau

Wearing my Bart Simpson glasses on the boat

A happy fellow tramper at the start

*Some damp scenes
along the way*

Attractive scenes along the way

*At the Quintin McKinnon
Memorial Cairn on
McKinnon Pass*

As you can see, mistiness was the norm

424

Continuing along the Milford Track

People ignoring the signs to get to the waterfall!

Milford

427

*At the end of the tramp, cruising on
Milford Sound with my brother Lawrie*

CHAPTER FORTY-THREE

Hump Ridge

THE BEST SUNSETS IN THE SOUTH ISLAND

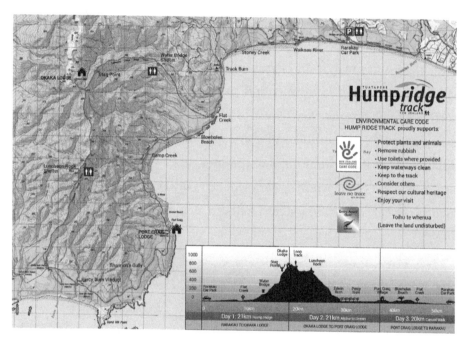

The Hump Ridge Track.

Map courtesy of Tuatapere Humpridge Track, humpridge.co.nz, March 2017.

THE Hump Ridge Track is just outside of Tuatapere, west of Invercargill. It is managed by Tuatapere Humpridge Track, a charitable trust set up via a partnership formed between DOC and the local community. The trust offers a range of tour packages such as guided tours and helicopter rides, and it is well worth consulting its website, shown above, even if you are just a more ordinary sort of tramper.

A three-day loop track along the south coast of New Zealand, the Hump Ridge Track covers fifty-five kilometres of beaches, forests and subalpine terrain.[98] The night before the tramp, I stayed in Tuatapere at a backpackers' hostel. Unfortunately, just as I was trying to get to sleep, the local youth began doing burnouts outside my window in their cars. There were people partying on the street and in the hostel until four o'clock in the morning.

After a patchy night's sleep, I started the track and soon met a cigarette-smoking businessman from Hamilton who threw his cigarettes in the bush as he was tramping. I also met and tramped with a Dutch girl who had been tramping around New Zealand for four months. The sunset on the first night was so beautiful, and you could even see Stewart Island in the distance. As well as witnessing the stunning views, walkers on the track can also cross some of the world's tallest wooden railway viaducts, though some, such as the Percy Burn Viaduct, have been closed for restoration recently.[99]

Hump Ridge Sunset

After completing the Hump Ridge Track, I returned to the same hotel in Tuatapere. The owner refunded my first night's fees and then gave me a free night and a lift to Invercargill the next day, which was a great example of southern hospitality and more than made up for my issues on the first night.

Once in Invercargill, I met the DOC manager responsible for volunteer hut wardens, who took me shopping. Here I was to get the food I needed for my next adventure: a two-week stint at the Port William Hut in Stewart Island at the start of the North West Circuit Track.

Hump Ridge

CHAPTER FORTY-FOUR

An Adventure to the Remote Stewart Island and the North West Circuit Track

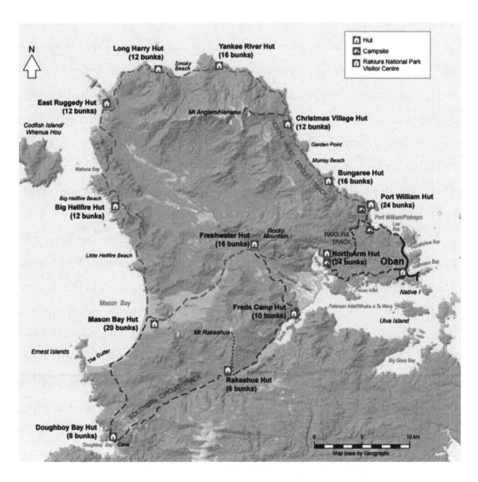

The northern part of Stewart Island/Rakiura, with Codfish Island / Whenua Hou at top left. (from DOC Brochure *North West and Southern Tracks*, Rakiura National Park, May 2015)

433

THE small size of Oban belies its importance as Stewart Island's only town and the entranceway to the North West Circuit Track where I was to be spending a few weeks volunteering as a hut warden. After catching a ferry over from Invercargill, I met Phil Brooks, the DOC manager in charge of volunteers. He took me through the safety checks, taught me how to operate the radio and detailed what was expected of me while at the Port William Hut, which I was to take charge of.

There were a lot of worried people on the island at the time, as roughly half of the DOC staff on Stewart Island were being made redundant due to budget cuts nationwide and a local review. Many of them had invested in the local communities and some also had young children who were part of these communities, so really there needs to be some government responsibility for supporting these people – a social contract of some kind. There was also talk of closing the North West Circuit on the island, which is a free camping spot for a lot of people.

From Lee Bay, five kilometres out of Oban, it's a three-to-four hour walk past Māori Beach to Port William Hut at the start of the North West Circuit Track. With a name perhaps referring to Fort William, a town in the Scottish Highlands, Port William has a very early European history. An attempt was made at logging in the area, but because of the area's extreme isolation it was hard to get either food shipped in to the harbour or logs shipped out, beginning a downward spiral of a flagging industry and dwindling supplies.

As warden at Port William, I had to clean toilets and sweep the hut. I also had to put out camp fires at the camp site, a two-hour walk away, as well as collect hut tickets. It wasn't demanding work – but somebody had to be there to do it.

I was at Port William during the 'Roar', which begins in mid-March. As such, there were many deer hunters staying at the camp and they tended to hang their dead deer from trees, which shocked many of the younger trampers. However, most hunters would ask the trampers if they wanted to try the venison, and they were usually very impressed with the meat's taste.

As well as deer, feral cats and possums were numerous on Stewart Island and the local DOC office was not doing enough to control numbers in my view. At the campsite, I noticed the possums were eating the campers' food so I took the initiative to lay three traps and straight away killed three possums. While there are some vegetarian wardens who refuse to kill possums, and taking a life is never easy, possums kill the chicks of kea and kaka as well as damaging the native bush.

DOC uses 1080 poison to control possums on Stewart Island, but only hand-lays the 1080 poison rather than doing helicopter drops. This satisfies the deer hunters, as a heli-drop kills deer as well as its intended targets. A controversial substance, 1080 is not used at all in some areas, such as the Wilkin and Young Valleys in Mt Aspiring National Park.

Despite these predators, kiwi survive in comparatively high numbers on the island. The Stewart Island brown kiwi comes out during the day and is known locally as Porky because it is stockier than its North Island cousin. The first night I was at the hut I spotted one with my red LED torch, and on my last night there I ended up with a kiwi sitting on my boot for a full two minutes!

As warden, I would instruct guests to use a red LED torch to view the kiwi because ordinary white light torches are more visible to nocturnal animals and may scare them away. If you have ever noticed, red objects look black in the moonlight to human beings, because dark-adapted eyes generally cannot perceive the colour red and only respond to the blue-green end of the spectrum. The eyes of nocturnal animals are permanently dark-adapted and do not respond very much to red light at any time. Therefore, a red LED torch will emit an invisible form of light as far as they are concerned. It might not be completely invisible to them, as invisible as infrared for instance. But certainly, it will be less visible than a bright white light.

I met many people from the Auckland Tramping Club and the Auckland Catholic Tramping Club while on Stewart Island and it was with the Catholic club that I saw sooty shearwaters or tītī, commonly called mutton birds, landing at night and going into their burrows. It was a magical moment. Strictly speaking the term mutton bird refers to the shearwaters' large, fat chicks, of which three hundred thousand are harvested annually by Ngāi Tahu: a number which is fully sustainable as there are estimated to be over twenty million sooty shearwaters nesting around New Zealand, mainly in the Stewart Island area. The chicks are cooked and preserved in their own fat in a semi-dried-out state, just like last week's mutton, albeit with a strong fishy taste. This is a delicacy in the lower South Island and you can even purchase mutton bird meat in the butchers in Dunedin.

The term mutton bird, or muttonbird, is not exclusive to New Zealand and has been applied to related species in Australia and Norfolk Island, notably the short-tailed shearwater or Tasmanian mutton bird, which is also encountered in New Zealand. In Australia, the aborigines have a tradition of harvesting mutton birds. In fact, this is pretty much a worldwide tradition, though strongest these days in Australia and New Zealand. In the old days, the British were keen muttonbirders, too, harvesting northern hemisphere species of shearwater. The scientific name for the shearwater, *Puffinus*, references the fact that in Medieval Britain a shearwater or muttonbird was called a 'puffin', both in its preserved state and on the wing. Confusingly, the British bird nowadays known as a puffin is entirely unrelated.

One night, a young Czech guy was drying wood on the outside of the wood burner and nearly set the place on fire in the process. I was close to losing my cool but I managed to contain myself. He explained to me that they only use coal, not wood, in the Czech Republic and so I had to show him where the dry wood was stored and why it is not a good idea to dry out wood on top of a stove.

Māori Beach

Patterson Inlet

Mutton Birds

The DOC office on Stewart Island tends to use volunteer rangers, and when it came to the end of my stay, I discovered that the next volunteer had cancelled. I was asked to stay for another two weeks, which I happily agreed to. Most of the time Stewart Island has a cool climate, but during February and March it can be a Pacific Island paradise: hot and sunny and ringing with birdsong of tūī, kākāriki and kererū. When I walked to other huts I could hear the sound of the fishermen's radios mingling with the calls of the birds. It was absolute bliss and I was more than happy staying longer.

Myself as Hut Warden

Oban (above); Beach scene (below)

CHAPTER FORTY-FIVE

Whenua Hou and the Few Kākāpō Left

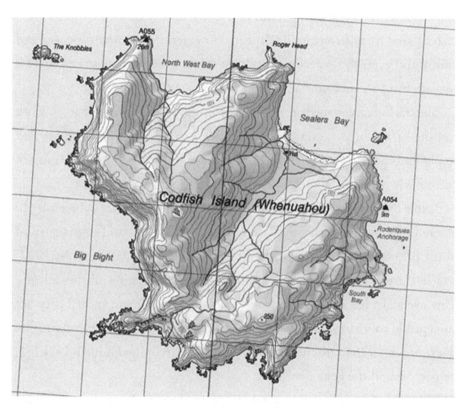

(LINZ via NZTopomaps.com)

A FTER my month on Stewart Island, I left for Whenua Hou, also known as Codfish Island, to work on track maintenance. To stay on the island, you have to go through quarantine; which I did in Invercargill. During the process, they checked for foreign grasses in my gear, so I had

441

made sure to purchase new socks and wash down my pack and wet weather gear.

Before departing for the island, I realised I did not know whether I was flying there by aeroplane or helicopter. I was petrified because in the 1990s I had taken a tourist helicopter ride at the Shotover (Queenstown) and I had felt like I was going to fall out of the sky. To my relief, we took a four-seater plane from Invercargill Airport. However, the weather was wet and windy and even the experienced pilot was silently sweating when we took two attempts to land on the beach.

The track maintenance on Whenua Hou was hellish. We were set to work ripping up seventy metres of wire-meshed boardwalk with crowbars and staple-gunning down plaster tread in its place – all this done in the rain, of course! My back just about gave out after doing it for five days.

While I was there, a sick kākāpō had to be taken to hospital in Invercargill, where he later died. Sadly, the Forest Service, New Zealand's conservation outfit prior to the forming of the Department of Conservation in 1987, had left it too late before intervening in the conservation of the kākāpō. This oversight led to the birds' very small gene pool, and means they are susceptible to viruses due to their lack of genetic diversity. However, the discovery in 1975 of 'Richard Henry', the last remaining Fiordland kākāpō, helped expand the gene pool.[100]

The kākāpō breeding season on Whenua Hou is a busy affair. It begins with the male kākāpō's booming song, a mating call designed to attract the females. Some males are successful at this, but for the less adept, artificial insemination is also being used. This is essential because some breeding-age males, like Richard Henry's son Sirocco, were hand-reared and now prefer human company to the company of other birds! Poor Sirocco may never mate with another kākāpō but he has other pleasures – he is famous for making out with Stephen Fry's co-presenter's head on a British nature documentary![101]

During the breeding season, rangers frequent the wooden walkways on the island for about two months, travelling between nests and monitoring the birds. Once they are nesting, volunteers camp outside the burrows and monitor the comings and goings of the parent. There are cameras placed in every nest to monitor the incubation period.

Once the eggs hatch, each chick is like gold. They are weighed, hand-fed and all the growth processes are overseen. I met some of the kākāpō juveniles during the day as they were being weighed. Hand-rearing does occur, but as it can affect their breeding potential later, it is preferable that they are raised in the wild. The success of a breeding season depends on the growth of rimu berries on the island, as these are used to feed the birds. Around Whenua Hou you see a lot of berry collection points. Though much effort is made to feed the kākāpō, the rangers tend to lose a lot of weight while on the job!

The conservationists are aiming to spread the population of kākāpō across three small islands: Whenua Hou, Anchor and Little Barrier. It is amazing to think that kākāpō once actually lived all through Aotearoa/New Zealand until only quite recently. How anyone could stand by and see a species almost wiped out is unfathomable to me. During the 1890s, one man called Richard Henry (the namesake of the aforementioned kākāpō) attempted to transfer a number of the birds to Resolution Island, where he was working as caretaker.[102] Unfortunately, ferrets and stoats arrived on the island in 1900 and decimated the populations he had established.

After working so hard, I did a lot of hiking around the island and took photographs of yellow-eyed penguins, Sealers Bay, and the view across to nearby Stewart Island. The DOC rangers had also asked me to work on the track foundations but I replied that I was not a carpenter. They were pleased with the rest of my work though.

When it came time to leave, we had to take the helicopter out because of the high winds. I silently freaked out, but let no one know how I felt. I was given instructions in helicopter etiquette: keep your head down when boarding and exiting, clear the landing area for loose debris, never approach the back of the helicopter because of the tail rotor blades and so on. We loaded it up and when we took off I was very relieved! Based on my much earlier experience, I had thought it would be awful, but to my surprise it was a far calmer ride than the aeroplane. I loved the flight over Stewart Island and we made a very smooth landing in Invercargill.

Whenua Hou,
transport and tasks

*Whenua Hou wildlife –
penguin and kākāpō*

Sealers Bay above and below, with penguin above – The aptly-named Ruggedy Mountains of Stewart Island can be seen in the distance in both views.

Whenou Hou

CHAPTER FORTY-SIX
The Catlins

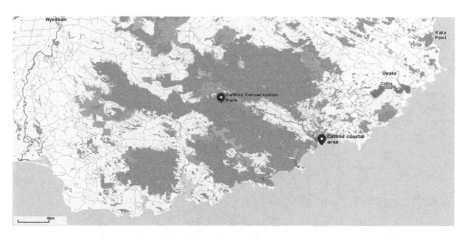

The Catlins, between Invercargill and Balclutha, with scale ruler (6 km).
(DOC Website February 2017; scale ruler relocated from cropped area of image)

C OMPRISING an area in the south-eastern corner of the South Island of New Zealand between Invercargill and Balclutha (south of Dunedin), the Catlins is a remote, yet beautiful, area. Straddling the boundary between the Otago and Southland regions, the region is sparsely populated, with its largest town, Owaka, only having a population of 400 people.[103] The area is notorious for its wild weather and is only warm for two months of the year in a good year – from mid-December to mid-February.

Despite its small population, the Catlins has a long history of settlement, being first populated by Māori tribes, who enjoyed the abundance of food from the sea and forest, around a thousand years ago.[104] When Europeans

My sister Maree spotting yellow-eyed penguins on petrified wood

arrived in New Zealand, several settlers migrated to the area for logging and farming. One of them, Captain Edward Cattlin, bought land off the Ngāi Tahu chief, Tuawaiki, a month before the Treaty of Waitangi was signed.[105] Although he only bought a small block of land, his modified last name now refers to the whole coastline between the Clutha and Mataura Rivers.

My favourite places in the Catlins are Slope Point, Curio Bay and a petrified forest on the sea at Porpoise Bay with rare bottlenose dolphins and yellow-eyed penguins. I went tramping at Papatowai, an inland coastal walk, where I fell into peat. Thank goodness it was summer and not raining, as I certainly would have been worse off in wet weather. Even then, I was up to my neck in peat. Somehow, I made it out and then headed to the coast following a rarely used track, where I cleaned all my clothes in the ocean and made it back to the car. Aside from the dangerous peat and beautiful views of the coastline, old Māori middens (camp remains) can also be seen along this track.

CHAPTER FORTY-SEVEN
Dusky Track

*The Dusky Track run northward through the middle of all this terrain,
from Lake Hauroko (bottom just right of centre) to the West Arm of
Lake Manapouri (top right).* (LINZ via NZTopomaps.com)

AFTER being made social secretary for the Auckland Tramping Club,
I resigned when I found out that neither I nor any other unattached
woman under fifty years old was allowed on one of their tramps to Dusky
Sound. Presumably there had been a scandal at some time and the ageing
membership of the club was determined not to allow a repeat. To my mind

453

such policies went some way toward explaining why the membership of this and other tramping clubs was, indeed, an ageing one. It meant that the ATC was not a place for young people to meet anyone, in direct and obvious contrast to the meet-up groups that the young people were joining! (This issue is the subject of a story in the July 2016 issue of *New Zealand Wilderness Magazine*, 'Smashing Stereotypes', which also mentions my crampon drama.)[106]

For want of a chaperone, I went alone to Dusky Sound to do one of New Zealand's hardest tramps, even though it is not recommended to go it alone. Dusky Sound is more than back-country, with no maintenance on the track at all, and huts with leaky roofs and full of mice and rats.

Trailing 84 km through the Fiordland National Park, the Dusky Track is a challenging tramp taking eight to ten days to complete and is rated by DOC as suitable only for experienced groups of trampers.[107] The track crosses mountainous country rising to 1,600 metres around Dusky Sound, a remote fiord named by Captain James Cook for the darkness falling when he first went to explore it (as I mentioned above, Māori referred to this whole region as Ata Whenua, or Shadow Land).

Starting from the eastern end, the Dusky Track is reached by means of a boat ride along Lake Hauroko from a bay on its eastern end near the foot of the lake, which can be reached by road from Southland townships such as Tuatapere. At a maximum depth of 462 metres Lake Hauroko is New Zealand's deepest lake and the Dusky Track starts at the head of the lake (foot of the lake means the end where it drains out, the head is the other end).

Local operators provide transport to the various points of access to the Dusky Track, which can only be reached by boat or by amphibious aircraft. But bookings are essential, and DOC can provide the details. The last thing you want to do is to end up quite literally in the middle of nowhere with no transport to meet you.

The track begins at Hauroko Burn Hut at the head of the lake, followed by a hike of four to six hours via two walkwires to Halfway Hut, the first of the huts on the track, followed by another three to five hours and two more walkwires to Lake Roe Hut. From here to Loch Maree Hut is the most scenic section of the route, a five to seven-hour tramp across the Pleasant Range with spectacular views of the Sound and the mountains around it, with another walkwire just before the hut. Trampers can then either head west to Supper Cove Hut on Dusky Sound via another seven walkwires, or north-east, the route which I took, to Kintail Hut, a walk of six to eight hours and one walkwire. From there, it is a steep climb through Centre Pass to Upper Spey Hut – about five to seven hours from Kintail Hut and two walkwires – and this is followed by a final stretch of tramping via three walkwires to the Wilmot Pass Road, which leads down to the West Arm of Lake Manapouri, where you can visit the famous hydroelectric power station.

I spent my nights on the track outside on a mattress, placing my pack in the mouse-proof toilets for safe keeping. As I was attacked by sand-flies throughout the night, I decided that next time I would take a tent. I pulled my calf muscle part of the way along the track and had to be airlifted out – finding at last that my personal locator beacon did come in handy!

I was preparing to bed down for the night with my pack and sleeping bag by the stream while waiting for the helicopter, but I didn't even have time to make a cuppa, as the helicopter arrived and winched me up above the trees by a good 50 metres. That was a memorable ride back to Te Anau.

Leaving the helicopter to stay at the hostel in Te Anau, I realised at reception that I had somehow managed to lose all my credit cards on the track. To make matters worse, I had been declared a missing person by the police, as Search and Rescue had not told the boat owner on Lake Manapouri that I had been airlifted out and, expecting me on their ferry, they had reported my absence. I was stressed out by the whole business including the lost credit cards and forgot to follow this up myself, somehow assuming that the boat operator would have been advised. So, it was a pleasant surprise for the police when they came checking for me at the Te Anau Hostel and found me there safe and sound after all, albeit with mixed feelings for the time wasted. In a situation like this always think: who might be expecting you? Still I had got out of one of New Zealand's hardest tramps alive, and that was the important thing.

CHAPTER FORTY-EIGHT
Te Araroa

Te Araroa, the Long Pathway

Sketched for this book from official sources.
Te Araroa does not yet officially extend to Stewart Island/Rakiura.

THE Māori word Araroa translates as 'long pathway' and it is just that. Te Araroa is a continuous, three-thousand-kilometre walking track stretching from Cape Reinga in the North to Bluff in the South (the pathway does not officially extend to Stewart Island/Rakiura but does so unofficially.) Along the way, it explores New Zealand's diverse environment with its plains, volcanoes, mountains, rivers, lakes and valleys. We are fortunate in

457

New Zealand that the meeting of the tectonic plates causes such a diverse landscape, along with the earthquakes and eruptions that have created it in more immediate terms and that are so unfortunate when they coincide with the location of a city (New Zealand gets earthquakes all the time, but most of them happen in remote back country).

In collision, the Australian and Pacific plates created the Southern Alps, a key feature of Te Araroa. Te Araroa becomes a journey, not just through nature and land, but through geological changes that have happened over millions of years.

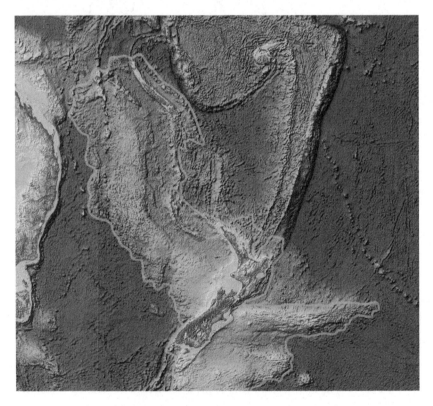

Topographical Map of the Zealandia Continent.
US NOAA public domain image, June 2006

As the map below makes clear, New Zealand is in reality the dividing range of a drowned continent. And so Te Araroa is New Zealand's equivalent of the Appalachian Trail, a similarly lengthy trail that runs the length of the Appalachian mountain chain in the eastern United States.

Te Araroa provides some of the best of New Zealand's tramping experiences. It would take five months to complete in full, but it is also possible to complete sections of the trail, which can be done in a few days, a week, or longer.[108] Many of the trail sections are also great day or two-day walks. Overall, Te Araroa is a very different trail from the traditional backcountry tracks that stick exclusively to the hills, as it connects settlements, townships and cities. Te Araroa is routed in such a way that trampers can be a benefit to the local communities by paying for experiences such as marae stays and other cultural experiences, or by buying food and paying for accommodation. The trail is designed to provide a wide variety of New Zealand experiences to locals as well as foreign visitors.

The Te Araroa trail has quite a history, with the idea of a walk stretching the length of the country being first discussed in Auckland in the late 1960s. In 1975, the New Zealand Walkways Commission was set up with a mandate to form a 'scenic trail' based on the Pennine Way in the United Kingdom, but found it too difficult. DOC tried again in 1995 and made it one of its goals in its Walkways Policy. DOC also proposed giving high priority to a network of countryside tracks crossing private land, as in the United Kingdom.

There are quite a few places in New Zealand where, from a road close to a town or a city, you look up to some ridge and wish you could get up there, or walk along it and look down, and think how good that would be for people's health and fitness – and yet you can't. That attractive range of hills is surrounded by private farmland and 'keep out' signs. Sometimes the farmers will let you across if you ask, sometimes not. In view of indifferent and capricious access nobody bothers to invest in the construction of a trail along the ridge-top even when it is, itself, in public ownership. Most New Zealand tramping has thus tended to be carried out in deep back country, a fact that suits the intrepid but not necessarily everyone else. The public is more or less locked out of many more accessible locations.

Unfortunately, DOC did not have the budget or sufficient co-operation from regional and local authorities to achieve either of the aims just stated.[109]

But today, the Te Araroa Trust (TAT) has at last achieved and indeed surpassed the goal of the great walkway, first set in the 1960s, with this beautiful trail: an achievement that has also expanded the range of accessible locations to tramp. Besides the trust, and the local authorities, there are also many volunteers who have helped to realise this remarkable goal.

There is just one major problem still to be solved, and that is the excessive amount of Te Araroa that actually consists of walking or bicycling along main roads, excessively close to speeding traffic. If this issue can be overcome, New Zealand will have a long trail it really can be proud of.

CHAPTER FORTY-NINE

Why not Swap Hiking Boots for Biking Boots?

N EW Zealand does not just have fantastic tramping and walking trails, but world class biking trails as well. I'm still making my way through them and they are too good not to mention.

The New Zealand government has spent NZ$50 million in upgrading and creating what they term 'New Zealand's Great Rides'. They are a series of twenty-three cycle trails in the backcountry of New Zealand and they are just that – great rides! These trails are considered New Zealand's premier cycle trails and you can expect them to be slightly busier than some of the others around the countryside. They are mostly off-road in nature. Not having to dodge traffic and pedestrians gives you a good chance to give your undivided attention to the beautiful natural landscapes on offer.

I have done some parts of the Great Rides system, which you can also pick up and leave off where you want. There are various difficulty levels, so there is a trail for everyone and anyone.

I started on one of these trails in Naseby, a small, historical goldmining town in the Central Otago region. The trail I did was about twenty-six kilometres of what I was told was the best scenery and track in the area.

As I made my way along the trail, I met plenty of people from all over the world. I was biking along and you would see people on their bikes with their luggage strapped down behind or in front of them. Others even hired bike trailers to carry their luggage.

It was something I thoroughly enjoyed doing, and will definitely do more of in the coming years. As I've said before, I do enjoy my own company but I wouldn't cross off cycling with a group either. There's something very leisurely about cycling around New Zealand. When you are away from the road it is a very peaceful experience, just gliding along.

Conclusion

W RITING this book has made me realise just how much more of New Zealand I need to tramp: the Wellington area, Christchurch and Te Araroa (The New Zealand Walkway).

I certainly feel privileged to have done what I have done, with all its trials and tribulations, and I love the mountains, lakes and many walkways in this country. It is important to escape immediate pressures, to 'contemplate the sublime' as philosophers say, and get back to what really matters in life. We also learn to appreciate just what a landscape we are blessed with.

That goes, of course, for the inhabitants of most countries, which have their natural attractions. But I like to think that it applies doubly in beautiful New Zealand. Furthermore, unless we learn to appreciate our nature and protect it, it may not be there forever. Some say we need to colonise Mars so that a few people will have somewhere to live when the earth is destroyed. I say it is important that we enjoy and protect what we have here, first and foremost.

I will continue to enjoy travelling, writing and the outdoors; completely loving that this is now my reality.

Acknowledgements and Thanks

I would like to thank my friends and family – you know who you are – and the many people I have met along the way.

Special mention goes to Nicki Botica Williams, who took many of the most wonderful photographs in this book. Additional thanks go to Nicki and her husband, Kevin Antunovich Williams, for sharing their experiences.

I would like to thank my editor Chris Harris, who also authored the sections dealing with urban areas including Towns, Traditions and Gardens in its entirety.

Any further errors or omissions that remain are, of course, all mine.

Did you like this book? If so, please submit a review on Amazon or Goodreads! For your interest, the front cover and introduction of the next book in this series, *A Maverick Cuban Way*, now briefly follow before the endnotes.

A MAVERICK
CUBAN WAY

Mary Jane Walker

MARY JANE WALKER

Introduction

C UBA is the Cinderella of the world, yet to realise its true worth. It's raggedy with a heart of gold, but at times glitters and has gold dust and rich carriages in the form of classic cars in bright colours. It is not a Western society. Expect the unexpected and it will happen. Batteries in the clockwork of time have stopped and it is like going back to the 1950s both in the cars, and in the shops.

Cuba is the sort of place I am drawn to. Why? Because I think you can make a distinction between travellers and tourists, and I consider myself within the first group. I like to go to the places less visited. There

The Plaza Vieja in Havana is worth wandering around for a refreshing taste of renovated Spanish colonial architecture.

is something about places that are just a little bit off the beaten track that gets the blood pumping and my heart racing with excitement and pure joy.

I love cultures, I love people, and I love getting to know them. The people in the hostels I stay at are more than just the 'staff' – they are mothers, wives, husbands, fathers and grandmothers, and everyone has their story. I have been travelling for a long time, my passion for travel ignited by my first overseas trip to Scotland to catch up with family.

Ever since, you will have found me somewhere different, and I have a long list of destinations planned. In fact, it is completely normal for me to be somewhere overseas and already planning my next trip. I have a penchant for travelling. Travel is my true passion, my love.

Cuba has always been of interest to me. I've heard other people describe it as laid-back, old-fashioned and hectic all at once. An island sitting amongst the rolling blue of the Caribbean, beautiful and complex, marked by history. And so, I had to go there.

Though I saw a lot and did more research for this book when I got home, I feel I've only scratched the surface. One thing is for sure: I'll be back!

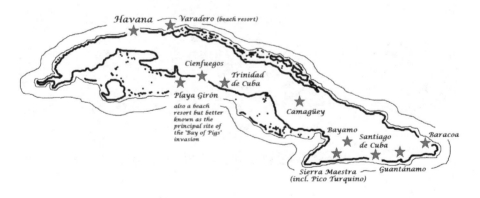

Places I visited in Cuba

Notes

[1] Karl Wolfskehl (1869-1948)

[2] Nicoll, D, & Mack, B. (2016, February 14). Fewer Kiwis doing Department of Conservation Great Walks. *Stuff.co.nz.* Retrieved from http://www.stuff.co.nz/travel/destinations/nz/76730875/Fewer-Kiwis-doing-Department-of-Conservation-Great-Walks

[3] Mitcalfe, B. (1961). *Te Rerenga Wairua: Leaping place of the spirits.* Retrieved from http://teaohou.natlib.govt.nz/journals/teaohou/issue/Mao35TeA/c20.html

[4] Department of Conservation. (n.d.). *Historic Cape Reinga.* Retrieved from http://www.doc.govt.nz/parks-and-recreation/places-to-go/northland/places/te-paki-recreation-reserve/cape-reinga-te-rerenga-wairua/cape-reinga/

[5] Department of Conservation. (n.d.). *Te Paki Coastal Track.* Retrieved from http://www.doc.govt.nz/parks-and-recreation/places-to-go/northland/places/te-paki-recreation-reserve/things-to-do/tracks/te-paki-coastal-track/

[6] Department of Conservation. (n.d.). *Te Paki Coastal Track.* Retrieved from http://www.doc.govt.nz/parks-and-recreation/places-to-go/northland/places/te-paki-recreation-reserve/things-to-do/tracks/te-paki-coastal-track/

[7] https://www.kiwisforkiwi.org/what-we-do/who-are-kiwis-for-kiwi/community-efforts/northland/

[8] Department of Conservation. (n.d.). *Te Matua Ngahere Walk.* Retrieved from http://www.doc.govt.nz/parks-and-recreation/places-to-go/northland/places/waipoua-forest/things-to-do/te-matua-ngahere-walk/?region=northland&park=1042601b-8d1e-461a-a8b9-866271df30f8&activity=walking-tramping#activitypanel

[9] Department of Conservation. (n.d.). *Waipoua Forest.* Retrieved from http://www.doc.govt.nz/parks-and-recreation/places-to-go/northland/places/waipoua-forest/

[10] Department of Conservation. (n.d.). *Tane Mahuta Walk.* Retrieved from http://www.doc.govt.nz/parks-and-recreation/places-to-go/northland/places/waipoua-forest/things-to-do/tane-mahuta-walk/?region=northland&park=1042601b-8d1e-461a-a8b9-866271df30f8&activity=walking-tramping#activitypanel

[11] http://www.ngatiwai.iwi.nz

[12] http://www.doc.govt.nz/parks-and-recreation/places-to-go/northland/places/cape-brett-and-whangamumu-area/things-to-do/cape-brett-track/; http://www.doc.govt.nz/parks-and-recreation/things-to-do/walking-and-tramping/track-categories/

[13] http://capebrett.co.nz/water-taxi/

[14] http://capebrett.co.nz/bookings/

[15] https://www.youtube.com/watch?v=OzvNMwurpPs

[16] Great Barrier Island Tourism http://www.greatbarrierislandtourism.co.nz/2015/02/09/national-geographic-gives-great-barrier-island-the-thumbs-up/ National Geographic http://www.nationalgeographic.com/travel/coastal-destinations-rated/top-rated/

[17] Department of Conservation. (n.d.). *A pest of plague proportions.* Retrieved from http://www.doc.govt.nz/documents/science-and-technical/everybodyspossum.pdf

[18] Great Barrier Island Tourism Directory. (2018, February 13). *Predators of native flora and fauna on Great Barrier Island.* Retrieved from https://www.thebarrier.co.nz/PDFs/Predators_Great_Barrier_Island.pdf

[19] Great Barrier Island Tourism Directory. (2018, February 13). *Predators of native flora and fauna on Great Barrier Island.* Retrieved from https://www.thebarrier.co.nz/PDFs/Predators_Great_Barrier_Island.pdf

[20] Great Barrier Island Locals Lobby Against Poisoning Pests. (2017, December). *Stuff.co.nz*. Retrieved from https://www.stuff.co.nz/auckland/100250911/great-barrier-island-locals-lobby-against-poisoning-pests

[21] Department of Conservation. (n.d.). *Rangitoto Island*. Retrieved from http://www.doc.govt.nz/rangitoto

[22] Department of Conservation. (n.d.). *Nature and Conservation*. Retrieved from http://www.doc.govt.nz/parks-and-recreation/places-to-go/auckland/places/rangitoto-island/nature-and-conservation/

[23] Tiritiri Matangi Open Sanctuary. (2010). *History*. Retrieved from http://www.tiritirimatangi.org.nz/history

[24] Te Papa http://collections.tepapa.govt.nz/object/199241

[25] Natural Heritage Collection, including photos by Dr Paddy Ryan, http://www.nhc.net.nz/index/lizards-new-zealand/tuatara/tuatara.htm

[26] Department of Conservation. (n.d.). *Bellbird/korimako*. Retrieved from http://www.doc.govt.nz/nature/native-animals/birds/birds-a-z/bellbird-korimako/

[27] Auckland Regional Council. (n.d.). *Hillary Trail: Waitakere Ranges Regional Park*. Retrieved from http://www.aucklandcouncil.govt.nz/EN/parksfacilities/walkingtracks/Documents/HillaryTrailWaitakereRangesRegionalPark-9Oct2012.pdf

[28] Ark in the Park. (n.d.). *What is Ark in the Park?* Retrieved from http://www.arkinthepark.org.nz/about_ark_in_the_park/what_is_ark_in_the_park.html

[29] See 'Timespanner visits Titirangi Village' (19 June 2010), on URL http://timespanner.blogspot.co.nz/2010/06/timespanner-visits-titirangi-village.html . This link contains a number of attractive photographs.

[30] See 'The Piha Tramway . . . ' (30 September 2015) on URL https://movin2newzealand.wordpress.com/2015/09/30/the-piha-tramway-piha-karekare-and-whatipu/ . In case this heavily illustrated link breaks, there is also a history of the Piha Tramway published in 1986, called quite simply *The Piha Tramway*, by D. Lowe (Henderson, Auckland: Lodestar Press).

[31] Auckland Regional Council. (n.d.). *Hillary Trail: Waitakere Ranges Regional Park*. Retrieved from http://www.aucklandcouncil.govt.nz/EN/parksfacilities/walkingtracks/Documents/HillaryTrailWaitakereRangesRegionalPark-9Oct2012.pdf

[32] http://www.stuff.co.nz/travel/destinations/nz/65533213/awhitu-peninsula-the-supercitys-bestkept-secret

[33] Auckland Regional Council. (n.d.). *Hillary Trail: Waitakere Ranges Regional Park*. Retrieved from http://www.aucklandcouncil.govt.nz/EN/parksfacilities/walkingtracks/Documents/HillaryTrailWaitakereRangesRegionalPark-9Oct2012.pdf

[34] Department of Conservation. (n.d.). *Historic kauri driving dams*. Retrieved from http://www.doc.govt.nz/parks-and-recreation/places-to-go/coromandel/places/coromandel-forest-park/kauaeranga-valley/kauri-driving-dams/

[35] http://www.thecoromandel.com/activities/must-do/the-pinnacles/

[36] Department of Conservation. (n.d.). *Kaueranga Kauri Trail (Pinnacles Walk)*. Retrieved from http://www.doc.govt.nz/parks-and-recreation/places-to-go/coromandel/places/coromandel-forest-park/things-to-do/kauaeranga-kauri-trail/

[37] Department of Conservation. (2011). *Family walks in the Waikato*. Retrieved from http://www.doc.govt.nz/Documents/parks-and-recreation/tracks-and-walks/waikato/family-walks-in-the-waikato.pdf

[38] Hamilton & Waikato New Zealand. (2016). *Te Aroha Mineral Springs*. Retrieved from http://www.hamiltonwaikato.com/destinations/te-aroha/te-aroha-mineral-springs/

[39] Department of Conservation. (n.d.). *Mt Te Aroha tracks*. Retrieved from http://www.doc.govt.nz/parks-and-recreation/places-to-go/bay-of-plenty/places/kaimai-mamaku-forest-park/things-to-do/tracks/mount-te-aroha-tracks/?region=BayofPlenty&parkId=77bdae7f-dae8-4748-84fc-c5957485c1ba

[40] Department of Conservation. (n.d.) *Pirongia Forest Park*. Retrieved from http://www.doc.govt.nz/parks-and-recreation/places-to-go/waikato/places/pirongia-forest-park/

[41] Walters, L. (2016, April 28). First White Island eruption in three years. *Stuff. co.nz*. Retrieved from http://www.stuff.co.nz/science/79400646/First-White-Island-eruption-in-three-years

[42] Quoted in Isabel McIntosh, 'The Urewera Mural: Becoming Gift and the Hau of Disappearance', *Cultural Studies Review*, Vol. 10, No. 1, March 2004, pp. 42-60, at page 43. Accessed on URL https://epress.lib.uts.edu.au/journals/index.php/csrj/article/viewFile/3520/3660 on 25 November 2016.

[43] McIntosh, p. 57.

[44] Barnett, S., & MacLean, C. (2014). *Tramping: A New Zealand History*. Nelson, New Zealand: Craig Potton Publishing.

[45] Watkins, T. (2012, September 12). Tūhoe deal puts bitter grievances to rest. *Stuff.co.nz*. Retrieved from http://www.stuff.co.nz/national/politics/7656493/Tuhoe-deal-puts-bitter-grievances-to-rest

[46] Gale, J. (2013, November 2). Finding their own way, together. *New Zealand Wilderness Magazine*. Retrieved from https://www.wildernessmag.co.nz/finding-way-together/

[47] Walker, M. (2017, June 21). 'Draft Te Urewera Plan focusses on "Living System"'. *New Zealand Wilderness Magazine*. Retrieved from http://www.wildernessmag.co.nz/.

[48] Barnett, S., & MacLean, C. (2014). *Tramping: A New Zealand History*. Nelson, New Zealand: Craig Potton Publishing.

[49] Barnett McLean, *Tramping*.

[50] Te Kahui o Taranaki Iwi Trust. (2013). *Taranaki iwi/history*. Retrieved fromhttp://taranakiiwi.org.nz/taranaki-iwi-history/

[51] Barnett, S., & MacLean, C. (2014). *Tramping: A New Zealand History*. Nelson, New Zealand: Craig Potton Publishing.

52 Leask, A., Theunessen, M., Backhouse, M., Martin, R., & Tucker, J. (2013, October 28). Trapped climbers die on Mt Taranaki. *New Zealand Herald.* Retrieved from http://www.nzherald.co.nz/nz/news/article.cfm?c_id=1&objectid=11147301

53 Robin Martin, 'Mt Taranaki – beautiful but deadly', Radio New Zealand, 5 January 2016. http://www.radionz.co.nz/news/regional/293493/mt-taranaki-beautiful-but-deadly

54 Sorrel Hoskin, 'Ian McAlpine – Mountain Man', first published 11 March 2005, http://pukeariki.com/Learning-Research/Taranaki-Research-Centre/Taranaki-Stories/Taranaki-Story/id/573/title/ian-mcalpine-mountain-man

55 Jeremy Wilkinson, 'Human Waste Problem on Mt Taranaki Summit', *Taranaki Daily News*, 14 January 2016, http://www.stuff.co.nz/taranaki-daily-news/news/75849207/human-waste-problem-on-mt-taranaki-summit

56 Helen Harvey, 'Cone of Catastrophes', *Nelson Mail*, 21 November 2007, https://www.pressreader.com/new-zealand/nelson-mail/20071121/282059092651497

57 Barnett, S., & MacLean, C. (2014). *Tramping: A New Zealand History*. Nelson, New Zealand: Craig Potton Publishing.

58 'Best in the World', *Taranaki Daily News*, 12 November 2008, http://www.stuff.co.nz/taranaki-daily-news/714539/Best-in-the-world

59 Eliza ('Mrs. Robert') Wilson, *In the Land of the Tui: My Journal in New Zealand*, London, Sampson Row, Marson & co., 1894, p.1. *In the Land of the Tui* is available now as free online scans on archive.org (by Google) and at the New Zealand Electronic Text Centre

60 http://www.teara.govt.nz/en/biographies/4m57/moncrieff-perrine

61 The website for Project Janszoon is http://www.janszoon.org.

62 Barnett, S., & MacLean, C. (2014). *Tramping: A New Zealand History*. Nelson, New Zealand: Craig Potton Publishing.

[63] Roberts, J., De Boer, E., & Wightwick, I. (2013). Heaphy Track Mountain Bike Trial: 2011 – 2013 [report]. *Department of Conservation*. Retrieved from http://doc.govt.nz/Documents/about-doc/policies-and-plans/national-parks/heaphy-track-mountain-bike-trail-report.pdf

[64] Kenneth B. Cumberland and R [Raymond] P. Hargreaves, 'Middle Island Ascendant: New Zealand in 1881', Part Two, *New Zealand Geographer*, Vol. 12, No. 1, 1956, pp. 51-74, at p. 69.

[65] André Siegfried, *Democracy in New Zealand* (E. V. Burns trans.), London, G. Bell & sons Ltd, 1914, p. 253.

[66] Gordon McLauchlan, *The Life and Times of Auckland: the Colourful Story of a City*, Auckland, Penguin, 2008, p. 13.

[67] In J. Rutherford, ed., *The Founding of New Zealand: The Journals of Felton Mathew, First Surveyor-General of New Zealand, and his Wife* 1840-1847 (Dunedin and Wellington, A. H. & A. W. Reed, 1940), from which a longer quote containing this sentence appears in David Hamer, *New Towns in the New World: Images and Perceptions of the Nineteenth-Century Urban Frontier* (N. Y.: Columbia University Press, 1990), p. 195.

[68] AJ Hackett Bungy Jumping. (n.d). *History*. Retrieved from http://www.bungy.co.nz/who-we-are/history

[69] As at the time of publication (Feb. 2017), this documentary can be accessed on Youtube under URL https://www.youtube.com/watch?v=HTacpRWl5ms&t=550s

[70] As of the time of publication (Feb. 2017), this documentary can be accessed on URL https://www.youtube.com/watch?v=NkTy6ogLDX8

[71] See, for instance Andrew McNulty, 'The Power of One', *New Zealand Listener*, 14 May 2011, http://www.noted.co.nz/archive/listener-nz-2011/the-power-of-one/; 'The Price of Heritage' (editorial), *The Press*, Christchurch, 28 September 2011, http://www.stuff.co.nz/the-press/opinion/5694123/Editorial-The-price-of-heritage

[72] See URL https://en.wikipedia.org/wiki/Cranmer_Court

[73] G. A. Bremner, *Imperial Gothic: Religious Architecture and High Anglican Culture in the British Empire*, c. 1840-1870, New Haven, Yale University Press, 2013.

[74] Bremner emphasises that there was, in fact, significant architectural feedback from the colonies.

[75] Debbie Jamieson, 'Would-be climber alarmed hired crampons fell apart', *Southland Times* / Stuff.co.nz, 11 December 2013, http://www.stuff.co.nz/national/9501281/Would-be-climber-alarmed-hired-crampons-fell-apart

[76] Hegg, D. (2010, August 6). *Mount French, 2356m* [blog post]. Retrieved from https://southernalps.wordpress.com/2010/08/06/mount-french-2356m/

[77] Burgess, P. (1967). The Wilkin Valley – December 1966. *Heels*. Wellington: Victoria University Tramping Club. Retrieved from http://nzetc.victoria.ac.nz/tm/scholarly/tei-Heels1967-t1-body-d15.html

[78] For latest tourism statistics, see Ministry of Business, Innovation and Employment (NZ), 'International Visitor Arrivals Commentary', 30 May 2017, URL http://www.mbie.govt.nz/info-services/sectors-industries/tourism/tourism-research-data/international-travel/international-visitor-arrivals-commentary

[79] Cropp, A. (2016, May 27). Tourism Industry claims DOC will be severely handicapped by funding cuts. *Stuff.co.nz*. Retrieved from http://www.stuff.co.nz/business/80469667/tourism-industry-claims-doc-will-be-severely-handicapped-by-funding-cuts

[80] Confidence and Supply Agreement between the New Zealand Labour Party and the Green Party of Aotearoa New Zealand, 52nd Parliament, 24 October 2017, Wellington, New Zealand; Section 6 (a).

[81] Department of Conservation. (n.d.). *The Rees-Dart Track* [brochure]. Retrieved from http://www.doc.govt.nz/Documents/parks-and-recreation/tracks-and-walks/otago/rees-dart-track-brochure.pdf

[82] DuFresne, J. (2006). *Tramping in New Zealand*. New Zealand: Lonely Planet.

[83] Department of Conservation. (n.d). Greenstone and Caples Tracks. Retrieved from http://www.doc.govt.nz/parks-and-recreation/places-to-go/otago/places/greenstone-and-caples-conservation-areas/things-to-do/greenstone-and-caples-tracks/

[84] Department of Conservation. (2011). *Routeburn Track*. Retrieved from http://www.doc.govt.nz/routeburntrack

[85] Johnson, D. (1995-2016). *Lord of the Rings Locations*. Retrieved from http://www.virtualoceania.net/newzealand/culture/lotr/

[86] Behind the Scenes with Bear Grylls. (2013, March 7). *Stuff.co.nz*. Retrieved from http://www.stuff.co.nz/entertainment/tv-radio/8393407/Behind-the-scenes-with-Bear-Grylls

[87] Department of Conservation. (2006). *Regional Economic Impacts of Fiordland National Park* [Report]. Retrieved from http://www.doc.govt.nz/Documents/conservation/threats-and-impacts/benefits-of-conservation/economic-impacts-fiordland.pdf

[88] Barnett, S., & MacLean, C. (2014). *Tramping: A New Zealand History*. Nelson, New Zealand: Craig Potton Publishing.

[89] Alpine Adventures. (2015). *Lake Marian, Fiordland National Park*. Retrieved from http://alpineadventures.co.nz/portfolio/lake-marian-fiordland-national-park/

[90] For instance, in the Nelson area. See Dent, B. (2015). Kea protection in Nelson Lakes. *Fauna Recovery New Zealand* .Retrieved from https://faunarecovery.org.nz/2015/07/28/kea-protection-in-nelson-lakes/

[91] New Zealand Alpine Club. (2014). *Homer Hut: New Zealand Alpine Club Hut Information Sheet* [Brochure]. Retrieved from http://alpineclub.org.nz/parkside/wp-content/uploads/2015/09/Homer-Hut-Information-Sheet-2014-update.pdf

[92] Jefferies, C. (2006). *The Darran Mountains: an alpine and rock climbing guide*. New Zealand: New Zealand Alpine Club.

[93] Barnett, S., & MacLean, C. (2014). Tramping: A New Zealand History. Nelson, New Zealand: Craig Potton Publishing.

[94] McLintock, A. H. (Ed.). (1966). Jamestown – A Ghost Township. An Encyclopaedia of New Zealand. Retrieved May 23, 2016 from http://www.teara.govt.nz/en/1966/jamestown-a-ghost-township

[95] Gunn's Camp. (2016). *History of Gunn's Camp*. Retrieved from http://www.gunnscamp.org.nz/history-of-gunns-camp/

[96] Gunn's Camp. (2016). *History of Gunn's Camp*. Retrieved from http://www.gunnscamp.org.nz/history-of-gunns-camp/

[97] Department of Conservation. (n.d.). *Historic Mackinnon Pass memorial*. Retrieved from http://www.doc.govt.nz/parks-and-recreation/places-to-go/fiordland/places/fiordland-national-park/heritage-sites/historic-mackinnon-pass-memorial/

[98] Department of Conservation. (n.d.) *Hump Ridge Track*. Retrieved from http://www.doc.govt.nz/parks-and-recreation/places-to-go/fiordland/places/fiordland-national-park/things-to-do/tracks/hump-ridge-track/

[99] Nicoll, D. (2015, September 29). $701,000 bill to repair Percy Burn Viaduct. *Stuff.co.nz*. Retrieved from http://www.stuff.co.nz/southland-times/72363389/701000-bill-to-repair-percy-burn-viaduct

[100] Kakapo Recovery. (2015). *Richard Henry*. Retrieved from http://kakaporecovery.org.nz/richard-henry/

[101] Williams, (2009, October 9). Frisky kakapo romps to fame. *Stuff.co.nz*. Retrieved from http://www.stuff.co.nz/technology/2946551/Frisky-kakapo-romps-to-fame

[102] Kakapo Recovery. (2015). *Richard Henry*. Retrieved from http://kakaporecovery.org.nz/richard-henry/

[103] The Catlins New Zealand. (2014). *About The Catlins*. Retrieved from http://www.catlins.org.nz/index.php?/site/climate

[104] The Catlins New Zealand. (2014). *Iwi*. Retrieved from http://www.catlins.org. nz/index.php?/site/iwi

[105] Wilkie, L. (n.d.). The Catlins Coast. *Department of Conservation*. Retrieved from http://www.doc.govt.nz/documents/getting-involved/students-and-teachers/field-trips-by-region/001-the-catlins-coast.pdf

[106] Hazel Phillips, 'Smashing Stereotypes', *Wilderness* (Auckland), July 2016, pp. 36-41.

[107] Department of Conservation. (2014). *Dusky Track: Fiordland National Park*. Retrieved from http://www.doc.govt.nz/Documents/parks-and-recreation/tracks-and-walks/southland/dusky-track-brochure.pdf

[108] Te Araroa Trust. (2016). *Overview and history*. Retrieved from http://www. teararoa.org.nz/overviewhistory/

[109] Barnett, S., & Maclean, C. (2014). *Tramping: A New Zealand History*. Nelson, New Zealand: Craig Potton Publishing.

Made in the USA
Middletown, DE
09 December 2018